Mormor

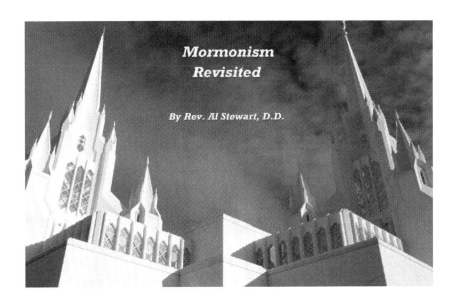

*Mormonism
Revisited*

By Rev. Al Stewart, D.D.

Pastor Al Stewart, D.D.

Foreword by: Dr. Daniel Mitchell

All quotations, notes, and sermons are mentioned with the source right at the time of usage so there is no need for a bibliography.

Special thanks to my dear friend Melissa Webb of Florence, Ky. for her hard work in editing and organizing this manuscript.

PO'BOY PUBLISHING

© 2017

Table of Contents

Foreword

There is one Lord, one faith, one baptism. Counterfeits abound. Many are deceived. Yet we are not without a witness. False doctrine will invariably show up in stark relief against that one faith that was delivered to the Apostles and has been embraced by the saints of all ages. When God is refashioned after the image of a false prophet and the Church is severed from its Head, the Lord Jesus Christ, we should know immediately that we are confronted with ideas contrary to the Gospel. Discernment follows knowledge as faith follows sight. The present volume offers a transparent assessment of a religious movement that purports to be a legitimate Christian denomination. For those who need understanding the present volume will be very useful. Pastor Stewart documents critical teachings of Mormonism that fail the test of orthodoxy. It is a bold yet amicable presentation of truth. Jesus said, *"the truth shall set you free."* For all who are deceived by this religious movement, or who wish to be able to confront its teachings, these short chapters will be most helpful. I commend this volume to the reader as one that will inform and gently prod you to effective soul-winning among the adherents of these troublesome teachings.

December 5, 2017

Dr. Daniel R. Mitchell, Pastor: Lighthouse Community Fellowship, Professor Emeritus of Systematic Theology, Rawlings School of Divinity, Liberty University

Introduction

You may be thinking to yourself: *"Do we really need another book on any of the Pseudo Christian Sects out there?"*

Well, my answer is a resounding YES! And the reason why is found in a principle based on a passage from the New Testament in 2nd Timothy 2:2:

"You, therefore, my son, be strong in the grace that is in Christ Jesus. And what you have heard from me in the presence of many witnesses, commit to faithful men who will be able to teach others also."

When I read this, I sense that each of us has been given by God a sort of *"sphere of influence"* if you will. Meaning that by using our specific gifts, whether writing, speaking or teaching, we can reach certain people that no one else can reach. I truly believe that! The book of Jonah shows us this principle. God gave this prophet a second chance after he ran because **he** was the man God choose to go to the great city of Nineveh. Perhaps God knew that Jonah would be the only one received by these people who were known for their brutal acts and evil deeds. Plus, each person brings a different view or angle to the table. It's like reading the four Gospel accounts. While for the most part they are saying the same thing, they each are coming from different angles. However when we piece it all together, we get an overall harmoniously detailed account of events in the life of Jesus Christ from these 4 different angles. The same thing happens regarding those of us willing to reach out to Mormons. Thus, I have no doubt someone *(hopefully a Mormon!)* will read this book and come away with something they never thought about or saw before concerning Mormon teaching and doctrine. So my prayer friends are this: that you will come away from my book with not only a burden for these wonderful LDS people, but you will also be more determined than ever before to go out and reach them. And remember this fact please: these Mormons will come right to your door! What a sin and shame to turn them away or worse, not have taken the time to try to love on and understand them! At their core they are a loving and caring people who value family greatly. Will you join me in this quest? I truly pray that you will as it's well worth the cost, for can anyone put a price on just 1 soul?

Al Stewart,

11/20/17, 11:23 PM

Chapter One

Pure/*White* & Delightsome

The Book of Mormon states in the second book of Nephi, chapter 30 and verse 6:

"And then shall they rejoice; for they shall know that it is a blessing unto them from the hand of God; and their scales of darkness shall begin to fall from their eyes; and many generations shall not pass away among them, save they shall be a pure and a delightsome people"

We will look closely later at this highly charged section of 2nd Nephi regarding race and ethnicity, a subject the Mormon Church has worked hard to move away from despite its documented history. But this *"white and delightsome"* [Note: The Printer's Manuscript, the 1830 first published edition, and the second 1837 edition have "white"; the 1840 third edition and the 1981 edition have "pure."] statement accurately portrays, at least outwardly an image many people have when they think of Mormons. This includes some of their practices like no drinking coffee, tea, or alcohol of any kind as well as strict adherence to a strong moral code known as the *"Word of*

Wisdom." And when it comes to families, Mormons take a back seat to no one! Families are a huge priority in Mormon society via their incredibly unorthodox teaching concerning *"eternal marriage sealing's"* so this is the image many have concerning the average LDS member or family and one they go to great length to give to the public via commercials and ads in publications, etc. They always emphasize strong families and moral living.

Having said that, this may come as a surprise to many, but the Book of Mormon is filled with many references to the idea that people of light or *"white"* skin are actually the good or godly people vs. those of *"darker"* skin tone. For instance, this passage from 2 Nephi 5:20-25 states: *"Wherefore, the word of the Lord was fulfilled which he spake unto me, saying that: Inasmuch as they will a not hearken unto thy words they shall be cut off from the presence of the Lord. And behold, they were cut off from his presence. And he had caused a cursing to come upon them, yea, even a sore cursing, because of their iniquity. For behold, they had hardened their hearts against him, that they had become like unto a flint; wherefore, as they were white, and exceedingly fair and delightsome, that they might not be enticing unto my people the Lord*

9

God did cause a skin of blackness to come upon them. And thus saith the Lord God: *I will cause that they shall be loathsome unto thy people,* save they shall repent of their iniquities. *And cursed shall be the seed of him that a mixeth with their seed; for they shall be cursed even with the same cursing.* And the Lord spake it, and it was done. *And because of their cursing which was upon them they did become an idle people, full of mischief and subtlety,* and did seek in the wilderness for beasts of prey. And the Lord God said unto me: *They shall be a scourge unto thy seed,* to stir them up in remembrance of me; *and inasmuch as they will not remember me, and hearken unto my words, they shall scourge them even unto destruction."*

These five verses without a doubt make it clear that the people known in the Book of Mormon as the Lamanites were *"cursed"* with black skin. Furthermore, it states the following about them: They were loathsome and that mixing *(meaning having sexual relations with them)* would bring a curse upon such a person who dared to do so. It further states they would become an idle people, and they would be full of mischief and subtlety.

I wish I could report that this is all the Book of Mormon has recorded in it as far as ethnic references, but there's more. A passage from 1 Nephi 11:13-15 states: *"And it came to pass that I looked and beheld the great city of Jerusalem, and also other cities. And I beheld the city of Nazareth; and in the city of Nazareth I beheld a virgin, and she was exceedingly fair and white. And it came to pass that I saw the heavens open; and an angel came down and stood before me; and he said unto me: Nephi, what beholdest thou? And I said unto him: A virgin, most beautiful and fair above all other virgins."* Another passage from 1 Nephi 12:23 states: *"And it came to pass that I beheld, after they had dwindled in unbelief they became a dark, and loathsome, and a filthy people, full of idleness and all manner of abominations."* This next passage from 4 Nephi 1:10 clearly promote the Nephites *(the white and delightsome people)* as superior to the Lamanites. *(the dark skin people) And now, behold, it came to pass that the people of Nephi did wax strong, and did multiply exceedingly fast, and became an exceedingly fair and delightsome people."* Mormon 9:6 states this*: "O then ye unbelieving, turn ye unto the Lord; cry mightily unto the Father in the name of Jesus, that perhaps ye may be found spotless, pure, fair,* *and white*, *having been cleansed by the blood of the Lamb, at that great and last day."*

The following is a discourse of Brigham Young quoted in its entirety. It can be found in several places, including The Complete Discourses of Brigham Young, ed. Richard S. Van Wagoner *(Salt Lake City: Smith-Pettit Foundation, 2009), 1:468-71.* This discourse is usually dated on February 5th, but was given on January 5th.This talk by Brigham Young, the second president of the LDS Church and a man every bit as influential as Joseph Smith, was entitled *"Slavery Because of the Curse of Cain."*

"The principle of slavery I understand, at least I have self-confidence enough and confidence enough in God to believe I do. I believe still further that a great many others understand it as I do. A great portion of this community has been instructed and have applied their minds to it, and as far as they have, they agree precisely in the principles of slavery. My remarks in the first place will be upon the cause of the introduction of slavery. Long ago mama Eve, our good old mother Eve, partook of the forbidden fruit and this made a slave of her. Adam hated very much to have her taken out of the garden of Eden, and now our old

daddy says, I believe I will eat of the fruit and become a slave, too. This was the first introduction of slavery upon this earth; and there has not been a son or daughter of Adam from that day to this but what were slaves in the true sense of the word. That slavery will continue until there is a people raised up upon the face of the earth who will contend for righteous principles, who will not only believe in but operate with every power and faculty given to them to help to establish the Kingdom of God, to overcome the devil, and drive him from the earth; then will this curse be removed. This was the starting point of slavery. Again, after Adam and Eve had partook of the curse, we find they had two sons, Cain and Abel, but which was the oldest I cannot positively say; but this I know: Cain was given more to evil practices than Abel, but whether he was the oldest or not matters not to me. Adam was commanded to sacrifice and offer up his offerings to God that placed him into the garden of Eden. Through the faith and obedience of Abel to his Heavenly Father, Cain became jealous of him, and he laid a plan to obtain all his flocks; for through his perfect obedience to Father he obtained more blessings than Cain; consequently, he took it into his heart to put Abel [out] of his mortal existence. After the deed was done, the Lord inquired for Abel and made Cain own what he had done with him. Now, says the grandfather, I will not destroy the seed of Michael and his wife, and Cain, I will not kill you nor suffer anyone else to kill you, but I will put a mark upon you. What is that mark? You will see it on the countenance of every African you ever did see upon the face of the earth or ever will see. Now I tell you what I know: when the mark was put upon Cain, Abel's children were probably young; the Lord told Cain that he should not receive the blessings of the Priesthood, nor his seed, until the last of the posterity of Abel had received the Priesthood, until the redemption of the earth. If there never was a prophet or apostle of Jesus Christ [that] spoke it before, I tell you, this people that are commonly called Negroes are the children of old Cain. I know they are; I know that they cannot bear rule in the Priesthood, for the curse on them was to remain upon them until the residue of the posterity of Michael and his wife receive the blessings the seed of Cain would have received had they not been cursed, and hold the keys of the Priesthood until the times of the restitution shall come, and the curse be wiped off from the earth and from Michael's seed. Then Cain's seed will be had in remembrance and the time come when the curse should be wiped off."

Brigham Young: *Journal of Discourses 10:110 (emphasis added)*

*"Shall I tell you the law of God in regard to the African race? If the white man who belongs to the chosen seed mixes his blood with the seed of Cain, the penalty, under the law of God, is death on the spot. This will **always** be so."*

And note, the first two presidents of the Mormon Church didn't just set their aim on the Negro race, but in this sermon, Brigham Young made this outrageous statement concerning the Jewish people:

Brigham Young; *Great Salt Lake City, Dec. 3, 1854. It was first published in Journal of Discourses 2:136-45 (142-43).*

"I'd Rather Preach to the Devil than to the Jews."

The following are references easy to look up which contain the same bigoted rhetoric:

Blacks Should be Used Like Servants (18 February 1855).

President Brigham Young, Delivered in the Tabernacle, Great Salt Lake City, Feb. 18, 1855. Journal of Discourses 2:179-91 (184).

Brigham Young: Blacks Will Be the Last to Be Freed from the Curse, 9 October 1859.

President Brigham Young, Delivered in the Tabernacle, Great Salt Lake City, October 9, 1859. Journal of Discourses 7:282-91 (290-91).

The following quote was so outrageous that it needed to be quoted in full.

Brigham Young: The Lamanites Will Eventually Become White *(8 October 1859).*

President Brigham Young, Delivered in the Tabernacle, Great Salt Lake City, October 8, 1859. *Journal of Discourses 7:335-38 (336).*

"You may inquire of the intelligent of the world whether they can tell why <u>the aborigines of this country are dark</u>, <u>loathsome</u>, <u>ignorant</u>, <u>and sunken into the depths of degradation</u>; and they cannot tell. I can tell you in a few words: They are the seed of Joseph, and belong to the household of God; and he will afflict them in this world, and save every one of them hereafter, even though they previously <u>go into hell</u>. When the Lord has a people, he makes covenants with them and gives unto them promises: then, if they transgress his law, change his ordinances, and break the covenants he has made with them, he will put

a mark upon them, <u>as in the case of the</u> <u>*Lamanites and other portions of the house of*</u> <u>*Israel</u>; <u>but by-and-by they will become a white*</u> <u>*and delightsome people*</u>"

Brigham Young: Curses on Blacks and Indians (9 April 1871).

Brigham Young, delivered in the New Tabernacle, Salt Lake City, April 9, 1871. Journal of Discourses 14:78-91 (86-87).

I trust you agree that this is enough evidence to show how early Mormon leaders had some very ungodly and unbiblical views on race and ethnicity. There is certainly much more I could of shared, however *"overkill"* is not necessary in proving one's point, I trust you agree, but know that there were many more quotes by other early Mormon leaders I could have included here. Blacks and minorities were not allowed the Mormon Priesthood until a *"special revelation"* came to President Spencer Kimball in 1978. It took a very **LONG** time for equality, at least on paper to come to the LDS Church far behind many other Religious organizations to say the least.

Chapter Two

Willing To Engage

Here's the great news, are you ready? Of all the Pseudo Christian groups around, I would say that LDS members are some of the easiest to engage as well as the most willing to talk. Now, I'm not saying by any means they are the easiest to win to Christ, they are not! But they are easier to talk to and seem to be more willing to engage. I think that their large family and communal structure makes dialoguing much easier overall. And remember as I have said and will repeat many times over in this book, Mormons really are good people! And here is the incredible part: they will literally come and knock at your door! I mean, wow! Could it possibly be any easier? However, it's going to be an uphill battle and it can take a very long time. The real question I want to ask is this: Are you willing to invest? This investment will include your time, as well as your willingness to become a real friend. It will take all of this and more. But sadly, the facts prove that most Christians are just **NOT** willing to make such an investment. As you continue reading in this chapter, you will hear some quotes from a former Mormon Missionary like

Micah Wilder who support's this claim. At Greater Grace Chapel where I Pastor, I am always quick to point out to our Congregation the following statement: *"Do not preach the Gospel to a person unless you are willing to make the proper time and needed investment."* Sharing the Gospel with a person is like building a bridge. It's not built overnight. It takes time! And the stronger the bridge is that you build to another person, the more weight it can carry. Over time, you can go deeper with that person. So yes, it takes time friends. For example, I recently had the honor of hosting Micah's powerful ministry to reach both Mormons as well as everyone. They are called *"Adam's Road"*. Founder and former Mormon missionary, Micah Wilder, in a talk made it clear that many of the doors he knocked on were those of Christians. He shared how most did not share the Gospel with him. Adding many were even borderline belligerent. I immediately thought of the Apostle Peter's words in 1 Peter 3:15: *"but honor the Messiah as Lord in your hearts. Always be ready to give a defense to anyone who asks you for a reason for the hope that is in you."* Another passage I think that lends credibility to Micah's claim that Christians are not making the most of these incredible opportunities that are at their own doors is Luke 10:2: *"He told them: "The* harvest is abundant, *but the workers are few.* *Therefore, pray to the Lord of the harvest to send out workers into His harvest"* How sad is this, friends? God is sending people right to our doors, yet we are unwilling to take the time to *"give an account of the hope"* that is within us! And I'm not only talking about LDS Missionaries here. Think about how many times a Jehovah's Witness has knocked at your door? Here in Lynchburg, I've even had people tell me that members of the Baha'i faith have knocked on their doors. Yet another example substantiating this claim is one I experienced back while going door to door *(something I do fairly regularly on Saturday mornings)* in 2013 when I knocked on the door of a Korean Pastor who was here studying at Liberty University's seminary for one year. Pastor Sheen began to weep as he realized I was a believer and not a JW or Mormon, and then through his tears he made this incredible proclamation to me: *"we have lived here in Lynchburg in this apartment for 9 months now and we've had all kinds of people knock on our door, but you are the first Christians to do so"* In Luke 10:2 Jesus tells us plainly that the problem is not the harvest, *(which represents the world and specifically the people in the world)* but rather the problem are the laborers. *(The ones who would be willing to go into the harvest)* I would submit this is precisely the problem we face today in the Body of Christ as a whole. George Barna reported roughly fifteen years ago that only one out of every ten Christians will ever lead a single person to Christ! If that is true and it may well be, that's appalling I'm sorry to say. So again, I ask who will go? Who is willing to *"stand in the gap"* and reach these people who have lost their way spiritually? My prayer in closing this chapter is that you will look at chapter 11 which is entitled *"Valuable Resources."* Please get a few of those books or DVD's and begin to read and study the history and doctrines of the LDS Church. If you do so, then you will be prepared when the missionaries come to your door. Preparing will allow you to have a deep heartfelt civil conversation with them. *(arguing proves nothing, it's not about who shouts the loudest!)* Also, go to chapter 8 entitled: *"How to reach Mormons",* that chapter has some practical methods and thoughts along with some good ways to have those civil conversations with them. And know that I speak from experience. *(I am an adherent to the old adage; a man with an argument is no match for a man with experience)* May our Lord bless you as you take the time to do this most important work.

Chapter Three

Blind Faith Really Does Exist!

I talked just a bit about this earlier. Often Mormons are the easiest target for critics of faith. And I'm sorry to report that there are some seriously valid reasons for this that we will soon examine. But we will first address if the Bible teaches whether or not we should believe someone or something in the face of contrary evidence as some would consider that to be the definition of faith. Now it is certainly true that sometimes absence doesn't automatically mean something is not true, but what I'm speaking about here is something much deeper, hard contrary undeniable evidence, not simply absence. Far too many Mormons continue to believe wild, outlandish unorthodox doctrines, statements and extra biblical revelations despite the hard evidence out there that many of them know exists concerning the veracity of those teachings and claims.

As I quoted earlier, The Apostle Paul told us in *1 Thess. 5:21* to *"test all things. Hold on to what is good"*

And the warning in *Galatians 1:8-9* is very strong and I should add that those of us who have a personal relationship with the Biblical Jesus view this verse as a *"special warning"* concerning Mormonism: *"But even if we or an angel from heaven (sound familiar?) should preach to you a gospel other than what we have preached to you, a curse be on him! As we have said before, I now say again: If anyone preaches to you a gospel contrary to what you received, a curse be on him!"* And it goes without saying that an Angel from heaven would never ever preach a Gospel that is in direct conflict with the Bible, yet the Book of Mormon, given by the *"Angel"* Moroni, is filled with contradictions when placed next to the Bible. Let's take a close look for ourselves; here is just the tip of the iceberg:

BIBLICAL RECORD vs. BOOK OF MORMON RECORD *(BOM)*

Bible: *At the tower of Babel the Lord confounded "the language of all the earth."—Gen.11:9*

BOM: *At the tower of Babel the Lord confounded the language of the earth except the language of Jared, his brothers, their friends, and their families. Ether 1:35-37*

Bible: *Christ's Church and the Gospel would never completely disappear from the earth, thus having to be restored. Matthew 16:18; Ephesians 3:21; Jude 3; Hebrews 12:28. The Word of God will "never pass away." Matthew 24:35; 1 Peter 1:24-25; Isaiah 40:8.*

BOM: *"the great and abominable church has taken away from the gospel of the lamb many parts which are plain and most precious....and ...there are many plain and precious things taken away from the book, which is the book of the Lamb of God." 1 Nephi 13:26, 28*

Bible: Jesus the Messiah was born in Bethlehem, not Jerusalem. *"Now when Jesus was born in Bethlehem of Judaea..." Matthew 2:1 (see Micah 5:2)*

BOM: *"And behold, he shall be born of Mary, at Jerusalem which is the land of our forefathers...." Alma 7:10 Note: Jerusalem is not the land, but is a city in Judea as was also Bethlehem. (see 1 Nephi 1:4)*

Bible: *Believers in Christ "were called Christians **first** in Antioch." Acts 11:26 (The following from Alma is long after Christ's ascension into heaven.)*

The book of Alma which is claimed to have been written in **73 B.C.** calls believers *"Christians." Alma 46:15*

Bible: Hebrews states that Melchisedec was *"without father, without mother...." Hebrews 7:3*

BOM: The book of Alma says that Melchisedec *"did reign under his father." Alma 13:18*

Bible: The Bible clearly teaches that the fall of Adam resulted in sorrow for all of mankind: *Genesis 3:9-19; Psalm 51:5; Romans 5:12*

BOM: 2 Nephi 2:22-25 states that Adam's fall was necessary for mankind to have children and therefore have *"joy."*

In fact, the contradictions are so plentiful; there is even a host of contradictions <u>within</u> Mormonism itself. Here are just a few of the many contradictions between LDS teaching and the Book of Mormon.

BOM: There is Only One God: *Alma 11:26-29, 44; 2 Nephi 11:7; 31:21; 3 Nephi 11:27, 36*

LDS: Testimony of the Three Witnesses; GOD THE FATHER IS ONE OF MANY GODS: *"...it is evident...that a plurality of Gods exists." McConkie, Mormon Doctrine, p. 576*

BOM: God Is Unchangeable; *Moroni 7:22; 8:18; 3 Nephi 24:6; Mormon 9:9; Mormon 9:19*

LDS: God Was Once a Man Who Became GOD: *"Mormon prophets have continually taught the sublime truth that God the Eternal Father was once a mortal man.... He became God...through obedience" Hunter, The Gospel Through the Ages, p 104*

BOM: God is a Spirit, not flesh and bones; *Alma 18:24-28; 22:9-11; 31:15*

LDS: God Is an Exalted Man: *"The Father has a body of flesh and bones as tangible as man's..." Doctrine and Covenants, 130:22*

BOM: God has always been God from all eternity; *Mosiah 3:5; Moroni 8:18*

LDS: God Has Not Always Been God: *"We have imagined and supposed that God was God from all eternity. I will refute that idea, and take away the veil, so that you may see..."-Joseph Smith, Teachings, p 345*

BOM: God dwells in the heart of the righteous; *Alma 34:36*

LDS: God Does Not Dwell in a Man's Heart: *"...the idea that the Father and the Son dwell* *in a man's heart is an old sectarian notion, and is false."* Doctrine and Covenants,130:3

BOM: Refutes Baptism for the dead, no second chance; *Alma 34:32-35; 2 Nephi 9:36; Mosiah 15:26*

LDS: Baptism for The Dead Is An Ordinance Of The Church: *Doctrine and Covenants, 124, 128*

BOM: Polygamy Condemned; *Jacob 1:15; 2:24, 27-28; 3:5; Mosiah 11:2,4 Ether 10:5,7*

LDS: Polygamy Is a Principle to Be Practiced In Heaven: *Doctrine and Covenants, 132:61, 62*

And again, these are only a few examples. Then there is the **MAJOR** issue of the DVD that caused quite a stir a few years ago: *"DNA vs. The Book of Mormon."* Since the Book of Mormon claims there were these two civilizations living throughout North and South America, namely The Nephites and the Lamanites, one is left to ask, where are there anywhere in these areas even a trace of those societies? The Mormon archeologist is a very lonely individual with little to do because he has no evidence to prove the claims of these so-called *"revelations"* and worse, the outrageous claim there is a DNA link between Native Americans and the Jewish people is so far-fetched that it begs for the many pages of

27

description that follows. The article below is entitled: ***"DNA studies on the origin of Native Americans"***

"Although theoretically possible that a group of peoples could have traveled across the Atlantic Ocean 2,600 years ago, such a journey would have been extremely unlikely to succeed. Even travel across the Atlantic 500 years ago, with much better technology, was extremely risky. <u>Through numerous scientific studies</u>, <u>scientists have concluded that Native American populations are derived from Asian populations</u>, who crossed the Bering land bridge during or near the end of the last ice age. Because of the vast amount of continental glaciers, sea levels were ~300 feet lower than today, which created land bridges between many continents that are now isolated by ocean. However, much of the interior of the North American continent was still covered with glaciers, preventing migration from the West to the East at that time. The migrating population rapidly spread South along the West coast, reaching South America within a few hundred years or less. Once the continental and Bering Strait ice had melted by ~10,000 years ago, return from the Americas to Asia would have been extremely difficult, with travelers having to cross the Bering Sea by

boat, braving the Arctic storms. Scientific studies examining the origin of Native Americans use several different genetic techniques. The fact that all the techniques lead to the same conclusions is extremely strong evidence that verifies the validity of the studies. These genetic studies can be classified into six major groups:

Y-chromosome

mtDNA (mitochondrial DNA)

Polymorphic Alu insertions

Retroviral DNA elements

Intestinal microbial flora

Domesticated animals

The Y-chromosome is the sex-determining chromosome found only in males. This chromosome is passed down from father to son, and so, records the history of descent along the male bloodline. Since it is passed down exclusively by males, there is no recombination on the chromosome, making the genetics considerably simpler than those found in the autosomal chromosomes, which recombine in each generation. These studies show that Native Americans share genetic Y-chromosome polymorphisms with Siberian

Asians. One study examined, a C→T transition at nucleotide position 181 of the DYS199 locus, which was found in all five Native American populations studied. The same polymorphism was found in two of nine native Siberian populations, the Siberian Eskimo and the Asian Chukchi. As a control, researchers examined the DYS287 Y Alu polymorphic element insertion and an A→G transition at DYS271, both commonly found in Africans, but found neither African allele in any of the Native American or native Siberian populations. A second study examined the major groups of the Native American founding populations.6 Haplotype M3, accounted for 66% of male Y-chromosomes and was found associated with native populations from the Chukotka peninsula in Siberia, adjacent to Alaska. The second major group of Native American Y-chromosomes, haplotype M45, accounted for about one-quarter of male lineages. This haplotype was found in the Lower Amur River and Sea of Okhotsk regions of eastern Siberia. The remaining 5% of Native American Y-chromosomes were of haplotype RPS4Y-T, which was found in the Lower Amur River/Sea of Okhotsk region of Siberia. These data suggested that Native American male lineages were derived from one or two major Siberian migrations. *An analysis of 63 polymorphisms* and 10 tandem repeat sequences were analyzed for 2,344 Y Chromosomes from Native American, Asian, and European populations.7 Analysis of these sequences indicated that three major haplogroups, C, Q, and R, accounted for nearly 96% of Native American Y Chromosomes. Haplogroups C and Q were found to represent early Native American founding Y chromosome lineages, while haplogroup R was found to come from recent admixture with Europeans. Phylogenetic analyses of haplogroups C and Q traced both lineages to an ancestral homeland in the <u>Altai Mountains in Southwest Siberia</u>, from 10,100 to 17,200 years ago. Another study examined eight biallelic and six Y microsatellite polymorphisms from the Y Chromosomes of 438 individuals from 24 Native American populations and in 404 Mongolians. The data showed that there were two major male migrations from southern/central Siberia to the Americas (with the second migration being restricted to North America). Age estimates based on Y-chromosome Y microsatellite diversity place the initial settlement of the American continent at 14,000 years ago.

Yet another study examined more than 2,500 Y-chromosomes of wide geographic origin for the presence of the DYS199T allele. The allele was found only in *Amerindian and East Asian populations*. A large worldwide study of over 300 men examined 32 Y chromosome haplotypes and traced the ancestors of *Native Americans back to Central Siberia*, primarily the Kets and Altaians from the Yenissey River Basin and Altai Mountains. Another worldwide study examined over 2,000 males from 60 global populations and concluded that the founder population of Native Americans had migrated *from the general region of Lake Baikal to the Americas*. Other studies have examined the pattern of migration in the Americas revealed through Y chromosomal polymorphisms found in different Native American populations. These studies have found a North to South gradient of increasing genetic drift in the Americas. *This is contrary to the Book of Mormon claim that the founding populations originated in either Central America or Chile*. If such claims were true, the gradient would run in the opposite direction. An additional study indicated that there was a west-to-east migration of Native Americans during prehistoric times, which would be expected if Asians entered through Alaska and migrated South and East". Suffice it to say, there is more than sufficient evidence to show the Book of Mormon's claims of such civilizations to be fabricated. However, let me now list the objections. As I know no matter what is stated here, some will sadly choose to believe that which they know not to be true.

Objections to the studies Haplogroup X

"The last haplogroup identified in Native American populations was haplogroup X, which is found in a small percentage of Native Americans. Although it has not been found in Native South Americans, it is present primarily in the Northeast U.S. Native American groups. Originally, it was thought that this haplogroup was exclusively from European ancestry. However, studies have shown that haplogroup X is found in Altaians from South Siberia. Subsequent work showed that haplotype X is an ancient marker that is found worlwide.32 Recent DNA sequencing of a 24,000-year-old skeleton from Siberia showed that population was an admixture of 14–38% western Eurasian ancestry and 62–86% east Asian ancestry with haplotypes similar to Native Americans. A more recent skeleton from the same location (dated to 17,000 years bp) showed similar genetics demonstrating that those populations persisted until their migration into the Americas. Therefore, the claim that haplogroup X might represent the genetic contribution of

populations described in the Book of Mormon is false"

Genetic principles explain a lack of Jewish markers?

Mormon apologists have cited possible genetic effects to explain the lack of Jewish genetic markers in Native American populations. Frequently cited are the founder's effect and genetic drift. Although the terms sound scientific and possibly could explain the contradictory evidence, there is not a non-Mormon scientist who would accept those kinds of explanations as being valid. Let's first explain the principles and how they might apply to these studies. Founder effects can result from one individual becoming the dominant ancestor of a population. In the founder effect, if that one individual harbors a significant mutation compared to the population he came from, the genetics would be skewed toward that one individual. Genetic drift results in isolated populations as selective breeding occurs, skewing the genetics in a particular direction different from other isolated populations.

The Lamanites were only a small group of people in Central America

Some Mormons claim that the Lamanites were only a small group of people who were geographically restricted to a particular location, such as Central America. However, other Mormon scripture indicates that the Lamanites are peoples on the North American continent. For example, Doctrine and Covenants Section 28 says that the city of Zion will be built "on the borders by the Lamanites" Several Doctrine and Covenants Sections indicate that Mormon leaders were to "preach to the Lamanites" At one point, the text specifically relates the Lamanites to the "Indian tribes in the West" and that at least part of this borders on the land of Missouri.

In addition to the standard works, the standard Mormon teaching book, Gospel Principles teaches that the Lamanites are alive and numerous throughout the Americas.

The Lamanites Will Become a Great People

The Lord said that when his coming was near, the Lamanites would become a righteous and respected people. He said, "Before the great day of the Lord shall come, the Lamanites shall blossom as the rose" (D&C 49:24). Great numbers of Lamanites in North and South America and the South Pacific are now

receiving the blessings of the gospel. In order
to claim that the Native Americans are not
Lamanites, one would have to admit that much
of Mormon scripture and that the official
current teaching are false.

Conclusions

DNA vs. The Book of Mormon Scientific studies
conclusively shows that the major claim of the
Book of Mormon that Israelites are the
principle ancestors of Native Americans is
false. In fact, there are no Native American
populations that share ancestry with Israelites.
Attempts to wiggle out of the obviously false
claims of the Book of Mormon and Doctrine
and Covenants simply invalidate large amounts
of Mormon "scripture.

In going beyond the DNA evidence, allow me
to add that not one coin mentioned in the Book
of Mormon to date has ever been found, not
ONE, think about that! *Alma 11:4-19: "Now*
these are the names of the different pieces of
their gold, and of their silver, according to their
value. And the names are given by the
Nephites, for they did not reckon after a
manner of the Jews who were at Jerusalem;
neither did they measure after the manner of
the Jews; but they altered their reckoning and
their measure, according to the minds and the

circumstances of the people, in every generation, until the reign of the judges, they having been established by king Mosiah. Now the reckoning is thus—a **senine of gold**, a **seon of gold**, a **shum of gold**, and a **limnah of gold.** A **senum of silver**, an **amnor of silver**, an **ezrom of silver**, and **anonti of silver.** A senum of silver was equal to a senine of gold, and either for a measure of barley, and for a measure of every kind of grain. Now the amount of a seon of gold was twice the value of a senine. And a shum of gold was twice the value of a seon. And a limnah of gold was the value of them all. And an amnor of silver was as great as two senums. And an ezrom of silver was as great as four senums and an **onti** was as great as them all. Now this is the value of the lesser numbers of their reckoning— A **shiblon** is half of a senum; therefore, a shiblon for half a measure of barley. And a **shiblum** is a half of a shiblon. And a **leah** is the half of a shiblum. Now this is their number, according to their reckoning. Now an **antion of gold** is equal to three shiblons." And have you also noticed there are **no maps** unlike the Bible in the Book of Mormon? The reason is because not **ONE** city has ever been found!

Consider this quote from the introduction to the BOM: *"It is a record of God's dealings with the ancient inhabitants of the Americas and contains the fullness of the everlasting gospel."* Members are encouraged to focus on the spiritual value of the BOM instead of the historical aspects. I think the serious lack of evidence makes it clear why Mormons are told to look at the spiritual value above all else.

Here is yet another quote: On July 29, 1978, the Deseret News published an article in the Church News section called *"Geography Problems" (p. 29)* that actively discouraged members from studying the historicity of the Book of Mormon because such efforts would prove *"fruitless,"* that differing theories regarding Book of Mormon geography would *"undermine faith"* and that any theories put forth by scholars were nothing more than *"personal speculations."* Suffice it to say, like the coinage, no BOM cities have ever been found or unearthed as well. An excerpt from an article by Janis Hutchinson states the following:

"Have the names of any Book of Mormon cities been discovered? The answer is, no. In contrast to the lack of archaeological evidence for the Book of Mormon, the evidence

unearthed for the Bible is impressive: From Abraham's birthplace, over seventeen thousand written clay tablets were found. Also, the Israelite/Caananite city of Lachish left inscriptions from 590 B.C. telling about the reign of Zedekiah, last King of Judah. In Jerusalem, writings have been found validating the name of King David. In the Egyptian Museum at Cairo, the Merneptah stele dates to 1224-1214 B.C. confirming the name of "Israel". There is also the 700 B.C. written account of eight military campaigns written by Sennacherib, King of Assyria. Also the famous Siloam Inscription of 700 B.C., confirming King Hezekiah's tunnel. Then, of course, the Dead Sea discovery and especially the Isaiah Scroll-- we could go on. Just look how much has been unearthed, verifying biblical names of cities and people! Because of the lack of evidence for the Book of Mormon, Mormon scholars resort to rationalizations. One explanation they give for the lack of evidence is that God purposely prevented evidence from being uncovered because He wanted people to accept the Book of Mormon on faith. Using this reasoning, one would wonder why God hasn't kept all Biblical evidence hidden. Fletcher B. Hammond, a Mormon, adds another rationale. The reason nothing can be found, he says, is because "the entire face of the land of Central America *[was] changed" due to the great destruction of earthquakes [at the time of the crucifixion], recorded in Third Nephi." This, however, is not so. Book of Mormon history continued 400 years more after the supposed crucifixion-destruction, providing archaeologists with* **stable strata.** *Thomas S. Ferguson, founder of BYU's New World Archaeological Foundation, confirms this: Innumerable excavations . . . in the time span [of the Book of Mormon] (3000 B.C. to 400 A.D.) reveal great undisturbed architectural structures, extensive relatively undisturbed ancient strata . . . right through the time of the crucifixion"* LDS critics maintain the BOM is a work of fiction created in the 19th century. Critics do not accept that the BOM relates an actual history of real people who came to the Americas and were steel-smelting, chariot-driving, Christ-worshipping, temple-building people multiplying into millions, **yet left absolutely no trace of their existence.** No archaeological, linguistic, genetic or any other evidence of Hebrew culture in the Americas has ever been found to support the existence of such a people portrayed in the BOM. The book also contains numerous anachronisms like horses, elephants, wheat, and barley, steel, silk, various types of swords, etc., that

scientist say didn't exist in the Americas during purported BOM times.

LDS apologists often suggest Book of Mormon archaeology is ignored by the general scientific community, citing that non-Mormon archaeologists don't look for evidence in the Book of Mormon. Therefore, they don't find any evidence. There is a non-Mormon archaeologist, Dr. Michael Coe who has been writing about Book of Mormon archaeology since he was asked to write an article on the subject for Dialogue Magazine in 1973. Dr. Michael Coe is the Charles J. MacCurdy professor emeritus of Anthropology at Yale University and curator emeritus of the Division of Anthropology at the school's Peabody Museum of Natural History. He is an expert on the Maya who inhabited the same part of Mexico and Central American where most current Mormon scholars say the events of the Book of Mormon took place. Coe was asked to write his first article on Mormon archaeology in 1973 by Dialogue Magazine. In the article he states: *"The bare facts of the matter are that nothing, absolutely nothing, has ever shown up in any New World excavation which would suggest to a dispassionate observer that the Book of Mormon, as claimed by Joseph Smith, is a historical document relating to the history of early migrants to our hemisphere"*

Dr. Coe was also interviewed by PBS for the 2007 documentary The Mormons. Dr. Coe did a fascinating three-part podcast interview with John Dehlin for Mormon stories. In this interview, Dr. Coe discusses the challenges facing Mormon archaeologists attempting to prove the historical truth of their central scripture and his own views on Joseph Smith. Podcast Link: (*www.mormonstories.org/michael-coe-an-outsiders-view-of-book-of-mormon-archaeology/*)

Another interesting anomalies found in the BOM are:

Jacob 7:27 ends with the French word "adieu." Since the Nephites did not speak French (which didn't even exist until centuries later), how can this be justified?

Joe Heschmeyer in his article: *"Animals in the Book of Mormon" writes:*

"Their Scriptures include reference to "all manner of cattle, of oxen, and cows, and of sheep, and of swine, and of goats" (Ether 9:18), as well as "horses, and asses, and [...] elephants" (Ether 9:19) being in the New

World prior to Columbus – none were. **This is pretty easily provable, particularly for horses,** since their introduction shortly after Columbus' arrival revolutionized the lifestyle of the Plains Indians and many other groups. The mental image we collectively have of Native Americans riding horses and hunting buffalo is an image only possible after Columbus' arrival. Their lifestyle prior was radically different."

If you'd like to read Mr. Heschmeyer's article in full, which ranges from honeybees and other animals in depth here is the link:

http://shamelesspopery.com/animals-in-the-book-of-mormon/

All this makes me think why the new President of the Church made the following statement on the BOM, do you think the higher authorities in the Church do not know the things I've written here in this book or any other book that exposes the everyday Mormon to the truth?

Chapter Four

I've Done More Than Jesus!

What an outrageous statement! You might be thinking to yourself did anyone in Mormonism ever say something as blasphemous as that? I'm sorry to have to say the answer is yes and I'm afraid the evidence is clear and incontrovertible.

Mormon founder, Joseph Smith, Jr. *(1805-1844)* claimed he was visited by God and Jesus Christ in 1820 *(which according to John 1:18 is impossible as this passage states that "no man has seen God at any time, only the Son who is in the bosom of the Father has revealed Him")* and later by the angel Moroni in 1823. In 1830, he published the Book of Mormon and founded the Mormon Church with six members. According to LDS scripture, *"Joseph Smith, the Prophet and Seer of the Lord, has done more, save Jesus only, for the salvation of men in this world, than any other man that ever lived in it" (Doctrine and Covenants 135:3)* A month before he was killed in a gun battle at the Carthage Jail in Illinois, Smith explained, *"I have more to boast of than ever any man had. I am the only man that has ever been able to keep a whole church together* *since the days of Adam. A large majority of the whole have stood by me. Neither Paul, John, Peter, nor **Jesus** ever did it. I boast that no man ever did such a work as I"* (May 26, 1844, *History of the Church 6:408-409).* While Joseph Smith is not worshipped by the Mormon Church, he is strongly revered. There is an LDS Hymn entitled *"Praise to the Man"* written in his honor. As thirteenth President Ezra Taft Benson said, *"Joseph Smith has done more for the salvation of men in this world than any man who ever lived in it, except the Master"* *(The Teachings of Ezra Taft Benson, 132).*

Remembering his December 23rd birthday, fifteenth President Gordon B. Hinckley declared, "*We stand in reverence before him as He is the great prophet of this dispensation. He stands as the head of this great and mighty work which is spreading across the earth. He is our prophet, our revelator, our seer, our friend. Let us not forget him. Let not his memory be forgotten in the celebration of Christmas. God be thanked for the Prophet Joseph"* *("Joseph Smith: Restorer of Truth," Ensign, December 2003, 18-19).*

Please take notice that both the D&C *(Doctrines and Covenants)* and President Benson stop short of saying that Joseph Smith was equal to, or did more than Jesus; however that is not what Joseph stated! The original quote is as follows; let's look at it now for a 2nd time:

*"I have more to boast of than **any man** had. I am the **only** man that has been able to keep a whole church together since the days of Adam. A large majority of the whole have stood by me. <u>Neither Paul,</u> <u>John,</u> <u>Peter nor **Jesus** ever did it</u>. I boast that **no man** ever did such a work as I. **<u>The followers of Jesus ran away from him,</u> <u>but the Latter-day Saints never ran away from me yet</u>.*" ("History of the Church", Vol. 6, pp. 408-409, 1884).*

This statement is heretical and blasphemous. For any human to claim they have done more than the only one who was able to be the propitiation *(acceptable sacrifice)* at Calvary, as He freely gave His life for all humanity, is incredibly outrageous and this statement alone should cause **EVERY** Latter-Day Saint to flee the Mormon Church post haste period. I have yet to have a conversation *(and I've had many)* with any Mormon who didn't either express disgust or try to quickly circumvent this statement. I must give credit where it's due to those LDS members who recognize that this statement was made in error. Sadly, far too many will stop short of leaving, even after learning their founder said this. That cannot be justified. Each LDS member who hears this and remains will indeed be held accountable for what they choose to ignore. Usually the common thought process with things like this is, *"okay if this is wrong, then what else did Joseph Smith say that is outrageous, false or just plain wrong?"* Well, let's take a closer look to see the undeniable recorded record. Let it speak for itself whether this man was a Prophet of God or not!

Unparalleled Destruction Prophesied:

*"And now I am prepared to say **by the authority of Jesus Christ**, that **not many years shall pass away** before the United States shall present such a scene of bloodshed as has not a parallel in the history of our nation: pestilence, hail, famine, and earthquake will sweep the wicked of this generation from off the face of the land....therefore I declare unto you the warning which the Lord has commanded me to declare unto this generation, remembering that the eyes of my Maker are upon me, and that to him **I am accountable for every word I say**....."—Joseph Smith, **1833,** Teachings of the Prophet Joseph Smith, 1976, p. 17*

Friends, this simply never happened. So now one must now ask the following questions:

1) Then by whose authority did Smith speak as it obviously wasn't by Jesus Christ?

2) Joseph Smith stated: *"Not many years shall pass away"* back in 1833 and now it is nearing the end of 2017, so some 184 years have passed already!

3) Joseph Smith said he is accountable for every word he says, so this clearly makes him a false Prophet according to Deut. 18:20.

Another overblown incredible statement that Joseph Smith stated was as follows: *"that the Book of Mormon was the **most correct of any book on earth**, and the keystone of our religion, and a man would get nearer to God by abiding by its precepts, than by **any other book**" (History of the Church, vol. 4, p. 461).* And take close notice of his statement *"any other book"*, as this would obviously include the Bible would it not?

So let us now look at his first claim that the BOM is the *"most correct"* of any book on Earth. Can it be true? The **facts** are as follows:

3,913 Changes in the Book of Mormon Paperback – 1996 by Jerald and Sandra Tanner *(Authors)* this book goes in depth from the first edition of the Book of Mormon from 1830. *(see photos on next 3 pages)* A photo-reprint of the original 1830 edition of the Book of Mormon with all changes marked, *(compared to a 1964 edition)* contains a 16-page introduction by Jerald and Sandra Tanner which shows that the changes are not in harmony with the original text. The evidence shows that over 3,900 changes have been made, actually 3,913 to be exact to the *"most correct book on earth"*

This book can be purchased through:

Utah Lighthouse Ministry

PO Box 1884, Salt Lake City, UT 84110

Please notice the following exhibits:

3,913 Changes in the Book of Mormon

THE

BOOK OF MORMON:

AN ACCOUNT WRITTEN BY THE HAND OF MOR-
MON, UPON PLATES TAKEN FROM
THE PLATES OF NEPHI.

Wherefore it is an abridgment of the Record of the People of Nephi; and also of the Lamanites; written to the Lamanites, which are a remnant of the House of Israel; and also to Jew and Gentile; written by way of commandment, and also by the spirit of Prophesy and of Revelation. Written, and sealed up, and hid up unto the Lord, that they might not be destroyed; to come forth by the gift and power of God unto the interpretation thereof; sealed by the hand of Moroni, and hid up unto the Lord, to come forth in due time by the way of Gentile; the interpretation thereof by the gift of God; an abridgment taken from the Book of Ether.

Also, which is a Record of the People of Jared, which were scattered at the time the Lord confounded the language of the people when they were building a tower to get to Heaven; which is to show unto the remnant of the House of Israel how great things the Lord hath done for their fathers; and that they may know the covenants of the Lord, that they are not cast off forever; and also to the convincing of the Jew and Gentile that Jesus is the Christ, the Eternal God, manifesting Himself unto all nations. And now if there be fault, it be the mistake of men; wherefore condemn not the things of God, that ye may be found spotless at the judgment seat of Christ.

BY JOSEPH SMITH, JUNIOR,
AUTHOR AND PROPRIETOR.

PALMYRA:
PRINTED BY E. B. GRANDIN, FOR THE AUTHOR.
1830.

*A Photo Reprint of the Original 1830 Edition of
The Book of Mormon With the Changes Marked*

By Jerald and Sandra Tanner

Chart to Locate 1981 Book of Mormon Verses
in the Original 1830 Book of Mormon

Since the original 1830 Book of Mormon did not have verses, and had different chapter divisions, this chart will aid in finding current Book of Mormon verses in the 1830 Book of Mormon.

Utah Lighthouse Ministry – P.O. Box 1884 – Salt Lake City, UT 84110   www.utlm.org

1830 Page	1981 Verses	1830 Page	1981 Verses	1830 Page	1981 Verses	1830 Page	1981 Verses
1	First Page	71	2 Nephi 4:33-5:7	141	Jacob 7:5-16	211	Mosiah 26:29-27:3
2	Page Deleted	72	2 Nephi 5:7-20	142	Jacob 7:16-26	212	Mosiah 27:3-14
3	Preface Deleted	73	2 Nephi 5:20-34	143	Jacob 7:26-Enos 1:10	213	Mosiah 27:14-24
4	Preface Deleted	74	2 Nephi 6:1-9	144	Enos 1:10-20	214	Mosiah 27:24-35
5	1 Nephi 1:1-4	75	2 Nephi 6:9-7:1	145	Enos 1:20-27	215	Mosiah 27:35-28:7
6	1 Nephi 1:5-16	76	2 Nephi 7:1-8:3	146	Jarom 1:1-7	216	Mosiah 28:7-19
7	1 Nephi 1:16-2:5	77	2 Nephi 8:4-18	147	Jarom 1:7-15	217	Mosiah 28:20-29:11
8	1 Nephi 2:5-16	78	2 Nephi 8:18-9:5	148	Omni 1:1-9	218	Mosiah 29:11-22
9	1 Nephi 2:16-3:7	79	2 Nephi 9:5-12	149	Omni 1:9-17	219	Mosiah 29:22-33
10	1 Nephi 3:7-20	80	2 Nephi 9:13-21	150	Omni 1:17-26	220	Mosiah 29:33-44
11	1 Nephi 3:21-4:2	81	2 Nephi 9:21-35	151	Omni 1:27-W o M 1:4	221	Mosiah29:44-Alma1:4
12	1 Nephi 4:2-17	82	2 Nephi 9:36-46	152	Words of Mor. 1:4-14	222	Alma 1:4-15
13	1 Nephi 4:17-32	83	2 Nephi 9:46-10:1	153	W o M 1:14-Mosiah1:4	223	Alma 1:15-26
14	1 Nephi 4:32-5:7	84	2 Nephi 10:2-15	154	Mosiah 1:4-11	224	Alma 1:26-2:2
15	1 Nephi 5:7-20	85	2 Nephi 10:15-25	155	Mosiah 1:12-2:4	225	Alma 2:2-16
16	1 Nephi 5:20-7:4	86	2 Nephi 11:1-12:4	156	Mosiah 2:4-12	226	Alma 2:16-27
17	1 Nephi 7:5-16	87	2 Nephi 12:4-21	157	Mosiah 2:12-22	227	Alma 2:27-3:1
18	1 Nephi 7:16-8:4	88	2 Nephi 12:21-13:17	158	Mosiah 2:23-33	228	Alma 3:1-13
19	1 Nephi 8:5-21	89	2 Nephi 13:17-15:4	159	Mosiah 2:33-41	229	Alma 3:13-27
20	1 Nephi 8:21-36	90	2 Nephi 15:4-22	160	Mosiah 2:41-3:12	230	Alma 3:27-4:8
21	1 Nephi 8:36-10:1	91	2 Nephi 15:22-16:6	161	Mosiah 3:12-22	231	Alma 4:8-17
22	1 Nephi 10:2-13	92	2 Nephi 16:6-17:11	162	Mosiah 3:22-4:4	232	Alma 4:17-5:5
23	1 Nephi 10:13-11:1	93	2 Nephi 17:11-18:4	163	Mosiah 4:4-12	233	Alma 5:5-16
24	1 Nephi 11:1-16	94	2 Nephi 18:4-22	164	Mosiah 4:12-22	234	Alma 5:16-27
25	1 Nephi 11:16-31	95	2 Nephi 18:22-19:17	165	Mosiah 4:22-30	235	Alma 5:27-41
26	1 Nephi 11:31-12:4	96	2 Nephi 19:17-20:13	166	Mosiah 5:1-10	236	Alma 5:41-50
27	1 Nephi 12:4-17	97	2 Nephi 20:13-30	167	Mosiah 5:10-6:3	237	Alma 5:50-59
28	1 Nephi 12:17-13:8	98	2 Nephi 20:30-21:14	168	Mosiah 6:3-7:7	238	Alma 5:59-6:7
29	1 Nephi 13:9-23	99	2 Nephi 21:14-23:8	169	Mosiah 7:7-16	239	Alma 6:7-7:6

Exhibit 1

then will he remember the isles of the sea; yea, and all the people who are of the House of Israel, will I gather in, saith the Lord, according to the words of the Prophet Zenos, from the four quarters of the earth; yea, and all the earth shall see the salvation of the Lord, saith the prophet; every nation, kindred, tongue, and people, shall be blessed.

And I, Nephi, have written these things unto my people, that perhaps I might persuade them that they would remember the Lord their Redeemer; wherefore, I speak unto all the House of Israel, if it so be that they should obtain these things. For behold, I have workings in the spirit, which doth weary me, even that all my joints are weak, for those who are at Jerusalem; for had not the Lord been merciful, to show unto me concerning them, even as he had prophets of old, he surely did show unto the prophets of old, all things concerning them; and also, he did show unto many, concerning us; wherefore, it must needs be, that we know concerning them, for they are written upon the plates of brass.

CHAPTER VI.

Now it came to pass that I, Nephi, did teach my brethren these things. And it came to pass that I did read many things to them, which were engraven upon the plates of brass, that they might know concerning the doings of the Lord in other lands, among people of old. And I did read many things unto them, which were written in the Book of Moses; but that I might more fully persuade them to believe in the Lord their Redeemer, therefore I did read unto them that which was written by the Prophet Isaiah; for I did liken all scriptures unto us, that it might be for our profit and learning. Wherefore, I spake unto them, saying; Hear ye the words of the prophet, ye which are a remnant of the House of Israel, a branch of which have been broken off; hear ye the words of the prophet which are written unto all the House of Israel, and liken them unto yourselves, that ye may have hope as well as your brethren, from whom ye have been broken off. For after this manner the prophet written: Hearken and hear this, O house of Jacob, which are called by the name of Israel, and are come forth out of the waters of Judah, or out by the name of the Lord, and make mention of the God

of Israel; yet they swear not in truth, nor in righteousness.—Nevertheless, they call themselves of the Holy city, but they do not stay themselves upon the God of Israel, which is the Lord of hosts; yea, the Lord of hosts is his name. Behold, I have declared the former things from the beginning; and they went forth out of my mouth, and I showed them; I did show them suddenly. And I did it because I knew that thou art obstinate, and thy neck is an iron sinew, and thy brow brass; and I have, even from the beginning, declared to thee before it came to pass I showed them thee; and I showed them for fear lest thou shouldst say, Mine idol hath done them; and my graven image, and my molten image, hath commanded them. Thou hast seen and heard all this; and will ye not declare them? And that I have showed thee new things from this time, even hidden things, and thou didst not know them. They are created now, and not from the beginning; even before the day when thou heardest them not, they were declared unto thee, lest thou shouldst say, Behold, I knew them. Yea, and thou heardest not; yea, thou knewest not; yea, from that time, thine ear was not opened: for I knew that thou wouldst deal very treacherously, and wast called a transgressor from the womb.

Nevertheless, for my name's sake will I defer mine anger, and for my praise will I refrain from thee, that I cut thee not off. For, behold, I have refined thee; I have chosen thee in the furnace of affliction. For mine own sake, yea, for mine own sake, will I do this; for I will not suffer my name to be polluted, and I will not give my glory unto another.

Hearken unto me, O Jacob and Israel, my called; for I am he; I am the first, and I am also the last. Mine hand hath also laid the foundation of the earth, and my right hand hath spanned the heavens; and I called unto them, and they stand up together. All ye, assemble yourselves, and hear; which among them hath declared these things unto them? The Lord hath loved him; yea, and he will fulfil his word which he hath declared by them; and he will do his pleasure on Babylon, and his arm shall come upon the Chaldeans. Also, saith the Lord: I the Lord, yea, I have spoken, yea, I have called him, to declare I have brought him; and he shall make his way prosperous.

Come ye near unto me; I have not spoken in secret from the beginning; from the time that it was declared, have I spoken; and the Lord God, and his spirit, hath sent me. And

Exhibit 2

Exhibit 3

The **facts** as you can see for yourself above reveal that this *"most correct book"* has undergone over 3,900 corrections and changes.

Consider the following questions from the article: *"Is the Book of Mormon the most correct of any book on Earth?"*

Keep in mind Joseph Smith indicated any mistakes were corrected as they were detected. Some LDS members claim the mistakes in the BOM were made during the printing process. This raises some questions.

1. Wouldn't Smith have compared the printed version to the original hand written version to see if the printed version had any mistakes?

2. How likely is it that the fraudulent passages, anachronistic errors and fabricated words appeared during printing?

3. How do the LDS leaders consider the information on this topic to be *"taken out of context", "lies"* or *"half-truths"* when it comes from current and previous versions of their own scripture which they consider to be the most correct book on earth?

4. When LDS members say things like, *"God has revealed this to me",* have you considered that you have been conditioned to believe as you do?

5. Are you thinking with your brain as much as you are feeling with your heart? Given the number and the nature of the errors, would you entertain the possibility that there is something *"shady"* about how the BOM came to be?

Here are a few of the many examples of BOM errors:

- In Jacob 7:27, the French word *"adieu"* occurs. But how could a modern French word have found its way into those ancient plates? This is additional evidence of fraud and presents grounds for rejecting the Book of Mormon.

- 3 Nephi 20:23-26, dated at A.D. 34, refers to Moses prophecy about the Christ *(Deuteronomy 18:15,18-19)* However, the writer unwittingly used Peter's New Testament paraphrase of this prophecy *(Acts 2:22-26),* which was not written until around A.D. 63. **This was almost 30 years too soon and thus, shows evidence that the Book of Mormon is a hoax.**

- 3 Nephi 15:21 is a word-for-word quote of John 10:16 *(from the King James Version)* However, this version is somewhat less than 400 years old. To make matters worse, the Book of Mormon even quotes the italicized word *"and"* was supplied by the King James translators. <u>Here the writer of the Book of Mormon unwittingly demonstrates his work to be plagiarism</u>.

- The Bible relates at the crucifixion there were three hours of darkness *(Luke 23:44)* However, the Book of Mormon states there was darkness *"for the space of three days" (Helaman 14:20,27)* Of course, this is a big difference. Which one is true? Can God be responsible for conflicting statements such as these?

This is just the *"tip of the iceberg"* friends. But suffice it to say, this is clear and hard evidence. Now let us address Joseph Smith's second claim in his statement concerning the Book of Mormon.

*"and a man would get nearer to God by abiding by its precepts, then by **any other book**" (History of the Church, vol. 4, p. 461).*

I remember reading a book way back in the early 1980's entitled *"The Mormon Experience"* The book started off fine by correctly giving proper respect to the Bible as God's Holy and true Word. However, by mid-book, I read the following statement: *"I came into my room to find my friend reading that grand old book of books, the Book of Mormon."* I'm sorry dear LDS friends, but you can't have it both ways.

The Bible is either God's Holy and trusted Word throughout time or it is not. Joseph Smith did not believe it to be the final authority in all matter of Faith and Principle by his own admission when he stated the Book of Mormon would draw a man closer to God more than **"any other book".** This is part of the reason why any faithful LDS member looks upon the Bible as being *"tampered"* with and as *"not to be trusted".* Past Mormon Apostle Mark E. Petersen said it best: **"The Bible is so full of errors; one can hardly believe a word in it"**

This is the reason for their 8th Article of Faith, which states they trust the Bible *"in so much as it is translated correctly".* I'll say it again; you simply can't have it both ways. History, Archeology, and Science have all led the way to show us the Bible can indeed be trusted. Along with the discovery of the Dead Sea Scrolls in Qumran, it can fully be trusted as God's unadulterated Holy and true Word. Nothing of the kind can be stated about the Book of Mormon and all other so called *"revelations".*

I'll just take a moment to mention the truth about the so-called *"Book of Abraham"* This papyrus is perhaps the most concrete evidence against the Mormon faith. The Joseph Smith papyrus, the source document for Joseph Smith's translation of the alleged Book of Abraham, was rediscovered in 1966 in the Metropolitan Museum of Art in New York. At the time of Joseph Smith's work in translating the ancient Egyptian papyrus, between 1835 and 1844, Egyptian hieroglyphics had not been deciphered, and thus, Smith's translation went unchallenged. With the discovery and cracking of the Rosetta Stone and the later rediscovery of the papyrus, Egyptologists have translated the actual text of the papyrus and found it to be an Egyptian funerary text. The actual text is from the **Egyptian Book of Breathings** and contains **prayers for the mummy with whom the papyrus was entombed, named Hor.**

There is a lot more I could go into concerning this topic, but again suffice it to say the evidence is overwhelming and can be easily researched on the web. Jeremy Runnells in April of 2016 resigned from the LDS Church instead of facing what he called a *"kangaroo court".* His statement below upon resigning is quite revealing:

"I am disgusted by the LDS Church's President Ivins attempts—multiple attempts—to place

me in the same category as murderers and rapists and child molesters <u>for simply seeking official answers to church problems</u>. I have done nothing wrong. <u>I just wanted the truth</u>. I wanted officials from the church to resolve my concerns and doubts. For those of you who are struggling with doubts, stop doubting the doubts. Cherish your doubts. Explore your doubts. Resolve your doubts. Doubt is the beginning to knowledge and wisdom. The only power that the church has is the power that you give them. Tonight, I took back my own power. Thank you"

A quote from J. Ruben Clark which I will use again later is worth placing here to close out this chapter:

"If we have the truth, it cannot be harmed by investigation. If we have not the truth, it ought to be harmed."

Chapter Five

It Actually Isn't About Truth!

What a strange title for a chapter in any book, but especially in a book about Faith. So what on earth do I mean by the above statement? I'll do my best here to explain exactly that. Throughout the years, I have had many conversations with LDS people, men and women alike. As you will hear me say throughout this book, if family and creating a community atmosphere along with morality were the keys to enter God's kingdom for all eternity *(not married as Jesus taught in Matt.22:23-30)*, then hands down the Mormons would win that prize. But the fact is that we do not enter God's Kingdom by creating anything. Truth is there is NOTHING we can do to somehow *"earn"* any type of salvation whatsoever as Christ has already done that on our behalf as 2 Corth. 5:21 clearly states: *He made the One (Christ Jesus) who did not know sin to be sin for us, so that we might become the righteousness of God in Him.*

So while those things I mentioned are indeed important, good and wholesome, the Bible has always taught that salvation comes to us by grace through faith as *Ephesians 2:8-9* states. This biblical concept is also bolstered by the words of *Titus* in his Epistle in *3:4-5*. Both passages are listed below to read before we continue:

Ephesians 2:8-9: For you are saved by grace through faith, and this is not from yourselves; it is God's gift— 9 not from works, so that no one can boast.

Titus 3:4-5: But when the goodness of God and His love for mankind appeared, He saved us— not by works of righteousness that we had done, but according to His mercy, through the washing of regeneration and renewal by the Holy Spirit.

These passages of Scripture establish that we can't work our way into Heaven period! After having so many conversations with wonderful LDS folks over the years, I have finally reached a conclusion, one that eluded me for years and I'll explain it now.

You see, for years I have poured out my heart to many LDS people and have gone over facts, not conjecture or mere biased articles, or things from former Mormons who have an *"axe to grind."* And those types are certainly out there and rightly so they deeply annoy LDS members. *(please note that if this applies then reconsider your approach and more importantly, your motive)* I reached out so many times only to hear something like this back: *"I don't care what the facts are or no matter what you say I won't leave."* I truly can't tell you how many times I heard something like that and how strange it was and still is to my ears! The good news today is that there is a clear move away from that attitude in large part due to the massive avalanche of evidence now available to the rank and file Mormon.

Am I alone when I say truth matters and it matters big time? Consider what Jesus Christ Himself said in a passage that usually gets us Christians in trouble:

John 14:6: Jesus told him, "I am the way, the truth, and the life. No one comes to the Father except through Me."

For those who understand Greek, the language the New Testament was written in, know the definite article exists here. This means Jesus said that He was the **ONLY** way, the **ONLY** truth, and the **ONLY** life. Therefore the latter part of the passage rightly states: *"No one comes to the Father except through Me."* The Biblical Jesus that is!

Jesus here again used the phrase *"I AM"* (Greek: *"Ego Eimi"*) which takes us all the way back to the burning bush in Exodus 3:14 when Moses asked of God *"whom shall I tell Pharaoh has sent me?"* Jesus was alluding to the fact that He has always been there and is true Deity in the flesh, God in the flesh if you will as John 1:18 so clearly states. To Christians this means EVERYTHING. If this *"trilemma"* is not true than all else is a *"house of cards"* and falls quickly. But Mormon leaders have long learned how to circumvent facts, and I must admit they have done so in an impressive fashion over the years starting from the very beginning. In the next chapter *"Circumventing Truth"*, I'll talk more about this. Mormons, and please allow me to say this as it's true, unlike Jehovah's Witnesses who have many members who have little or no College education, in great part because of their constant doomsday prophecies *(they have predicted the end of the world in 1914,15,18,25,41 and most recently 1975, thus the reason why higher education is always shunned due to the reason that the end is always near so why go to school or seek higher education?)* Mormons on the other hand aspire to higher education. Many Mormons are CEO's, or hold upper management jobs and are very successful in the business and medical worlds. These are highly intelligent people. So you may ask then what's the problem right?

If it was about seeking truth as you can see even to this point in the book, one may rightly ask this question: *"how could a person if these things are true remain with the LDS Church?"* My sentiment exactly! So there clearly has to be something else and trust me, there is. Here are a few of my thoughts on what those things are give or take a few as I can only speak for myself here:

- *Tight knitted families and circles of friends, thus the deep loss that will occur should one leave.* Unlike most within Biblical Christianity, Mormons do practice shunning, although I will admit that it is nowhere on the scale that JW's do. But still, it is an effective reason for a Mormon to *"stay the course"* as they run the risk of losing family and friends by dissociating with the LDS Church. We Biblical Christians would do well to understand this and take it to heart as much of their lives revolve around the LDS Church, Temple work, Relief Society, etc. Mormons often have much to be done and all on a volunteer basis.

- *Temple Marriage Sealings.* This is something Biblical Christians need to understand. When a Mormon couple is considered *"worthy"* to attend the Temple, they can then be married in an *"eternal marriage ceremony"* in the Temple so the new Mormon couples hope is to be together for all eternity! Death is only a temporary separation and when reunited in marriage after death, they then hope to be the *"god & goddess"* of their own world and to spawn children to populate that planet they are assigned to. I know this may sound awfully bizarre, but it is what we are up against when talking to *"worthy"* Mormons, which makes it much harder to reach them with the truth of Scripture and Jesus words concerning Marriage **not being eternal or even existent** as I mentioned earlier in *Matt. 22:23-30*

- *Inner Circles.* As with Jehovah Witnesses, over time Mormons begin to cling and stay close to each other, thus losing most of their close relationships with people **outside** their Faith. This is a very effective tactic used by almost all Pseudo-Christian Cults and Cults in general. Think about it, you basically give up your *"worldly"* relationships going in and over time they are replaced by members of the same faith. So if one decides to leave, who do they have to look to or to lean on? I recently heard a former Mormon and his wife say that since leaving the LDS Church about 5 months ago, they had yet to hear from just 1 person who was in their Ward! *(Ward in Mormon speak means Congregation as most Mormon meeting houses may have 2 or 3 Wards)* Very sad indeed!

- Last, and this is perhaps the hardest to overcome in some respects is the *"esoteric ethereal"* sense of being and pride to be able to say *"I belong to this small group who knows what only a few on the Earth today know"* This may sound like *"hogwash"* to some of you, but trust me that its true. I have heard countless people who have left the LDS Church admit that they were filled with pride, in part due to the *"exclusive"* work they did and how they were 100% convinced that it pleased God. *(especially Temple work)* And the *"companion"* to this is a sense of *"looking down"* on others and thinking that you are somehow superior or better. One only has to look at the incredibly boastful writings of Joseph Smith to see that such a *"spirit"* still lives in the LDS Church. They use terms like *"restoration"* and *"fullness of the Gospel"* as badges of honor. You better believe that a lot of pride comes along with that baggage! So please keep these things in mind friends.

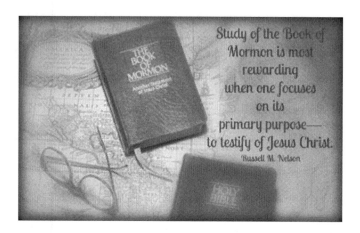

Study of the Book of Mormon is most rewarding when one focuses on its primary purpose— to testify of Jesus Christ.
Russell M. Nelson

Chapter Six

Circumventing Truth

Okay, so maybe your question is *"How do Mormons circumvent truth?"* Well a professional middle age family man recently said to me that shortly after joining the Mormon Church, he started looking around his local Mormon Ward and saw many well-spoken, well dressed professional businesslike people and confessed to me that he thought to himself *"gee these are intelligent people, this must be true"* But perhaps this follow up question is even more important as the picture above states for a very specific reason: *"Have Mormon leaders knowing that the evidence (especially historic and geographic) simply does not exist to support Mormon theology or the Book of Mormon created a sort of back* door path to circumvent the facts, even to the point that smart people are taken?" Well, let's take a closer look together at this question.

"A Burning in the Bosom"

Fair Mormon, an apologetically designed site in defense of Mormonism, writes the following on this burning in the bosom:

"It is claimed by some that the Latter-day Saint appeal to "revelation" or a "burning in the bosom" is subjective, emotion-based, and thus ineffective, unreliable and susceptible to self-deception. It is a fundamental misunderstanding or misstatement to say that the LDS revelatory experience is exclusively or primarily "emotional." The united witness of mind and heart is key in LDS doctrine. Even the body is involved in many instances, hence the use of language exactly like 'burning in the bosom.' The LDS concept of human experience is not one where we are carved up into separate, rigid compartments labeled emotional, intellectual and physical.

The LDS approach to human experience is holistic and involves all our faculties operating simultaneously and inextricably. According to LDS scripture, "the spirit and the body are the soul of man." (D&C 88:15) we are greater than the mere sum of our inner and outer parts. Ordinarily, it's not possible, nor is it desirable, to reject and shut down any one of our faculties. All of them combine to provide useful and valid ways of coming to know ourselves, the world, and God. All are involved in true spiritual experience.'"

The article goes on to say:

"Accordingly, a Latter-day Saint "spiritual" experience has intellectual content as well as emotional elements of peace or joy. In the early days of the Church, Oliver Cowdery received the following revelation through Joseph Smith: Verily, verily, I say unto you, if you desire a further witness, cast your mind upon the night that you cried unto me in your heart, that you might know concerning the truth of these things. Did I not speak peace to your mind concerning the matter? What greater witness can you have than that from God? (D&C 6:22–23). Notice the information is spoken to the "mind" and the feeling of peace accompanies the intellectual gift. Further, the solution for later doubts or concerns is not reliance on "a feeling" alone but an admonition to recall specific information communicated earlier."

Link:
(https://www.fairmormon.org/answers/Holy_G
host/Burning_in_the_bosom#Question:_Is_a_.
22burning_in_the_bosom.22_simply_a_subject
ive.2C_emotion-
based.2C_unreliable_way_to_practice_self-
deception.3F)

Mormon Leader Dallan H. Oaks states:

What does a 'burning in the bosom mean?'
Does it need to be a feeling of caloric heat, like
the burning produced by combustion? If that is
the meaning, I have never had a burning in the
bosom. Surely, the word "burning" in this
scripture signifies a feeling of comfort and
serenity. That is the witness many receive.
That is the way revelation works."

I could on, but I think these two quotes along
with the Fair Mormon article suffice to show
the appeal is made for one to pray, to seek
after a feeling of peace and comfort. In other
words, the appeal is you will sense this feeling
of peace and comfort come over you and there
will be a sense that these things really are
true. However friends notice what is
completely absent. Any appeal to the facts and
evidence that needs to be examined behind
such *"revelations"* like The Book of Mormon,

Doctrine & Covenants, or the Pearl of Great Price, etc.

What frightens me to death with this type of appeal is imagining for a moment a Christian Scientist *(which is neither Christian nor Scientific!)* handing me a copy of *"Science and Health, A Key to the Scriptures"* which is their *"revelatory"* manual. *(All Pseudo-Christian Sects have extra Biblical revelation due to the fact that the Bible does not support their unorthodox doctrines so they need to have other so called "scripture" to support those teachings)* And the individual said *"Al, pray about this book, see if you get a sense or feeling of comfort of heart and mind, etc."*

Oh my how utterly **subjective!** What a perfect set up for any person to be quickly led astray.

Here is a scenario you will never hear from Mormon missionaries, or from any Mormon: *"Al, we've come to you today to give you a free copy of the Book of Mormon (Missionaries never give out their other so-called revelations in 1ˢᵗ visits because they are trained and know fully well people would run away upon hearing such unorthodox doctrine before developing relationships, which bring security and community) and in giving you this free copy today, we'd like to ask you to please go online or to the library and examine the evidence for this book that was translated by our Prophet Joseph Smith."*

Guess what friends? That's not going to happen. The last thing that Mormons want is for a person to examine their history, doctrine and literature. Mormon Leaders like M. Russell Ballard, Neil L. Andersen, Jayson Kunzler and others have all made strong appeals to the everyday Mormon to simply *"trust"* their leaders. In other words, **DON'T EXAMINE!** Jayson Kunzler said if you are going to search, *"a Google search is not the proper place"* One must ask *"what are you trying to hide?"* As I quoted earlier, J. Rueben Clark states and I whole heartedly agree: ***"If we have the truth, it cannot be harmed by investigation. If we have not the truth, it ought to be harmed."***

There are many books one can find that bring out the facts to show beyond any question Mormonism is incredibly unorthodox as well as fabricated. This work is merely one of them, while offering what I hope is a bit of a different take as a few of my chapters are quite different from what you will read in many other books about the LDS Church. But I will list those books and DVD's that I think are most enlightening in the *"Valuable Resources"* chapter of this book toward the end.

Okay, so what does the Bible have to say about examining any or all claims made by any person or organization? Let's have a look.

Interestingly, the Apostle Paul when speaking to the Thessalonians about having a method for seeing whether something presented or spoken is true, said the following in 1 Thessalonians 5:19-22: *"Don't stifle the Spirit. Don't despise prophecies, 21 **but test all things**. **Hold on to what is good**. Stay away from every kind of evil."*

Notice what Paul told them, *"but test all things."* The Greek word used here is: *"Dokimazo"* which means to approve, **to examine the evidence for**, and to try **by meaning of investigating**. This is in direct conflict with the Mormon teaching of Dallin H. Oaks who stated: *"a feeling of comfort and serenity"* will suffice to show the truth. Where does the Apostle Paul say anything of the kind, or anyone in the entire Bible for that matter?

I'm also thinking of the statement made by Oliver Crowdery who received this from Joseph Smith: *"cast your mind upon the night that you cried unto me in your heart that you might know concerning the truth of these things. Did I not speak peace to your mind concerning the matter?"*

Again, nowhere is there any appeal to seeking out facts or evidence! I'm thinking I can go out tomorrow and start a new religion by simply claiming a revelation. Then I can tell people to just pray about it and do nothing else, as he did here with such statements in the LDS Church right up to today. Satan would undoubtedly jump right in the middle of that and have a field day!

In *2 Corinthians 13:5* Paul gives all of us a test believe it or not. He writes the following:

"Test yourselves [to see] if you are in the faith. Examine yourselves. Or do you yourselves not recognize that Jesus Christ is in you? —unless you fail the test."

So this verse is another passage of Scripture telling us to examine, to test. *(To my Mormon friends reading this book and I say friends affectionately, notice that to pass the test all that is needed is for Jesus Christ to be in you. No mention is made of having to do secret temple rituals, nor is there any mention of "after all we can do" and the reason that is not there is because Jesus already did the "all!")*

May all glory, honor and praise be unto Him! Praise to the Lamb, not to the man!

Richard T. Ritenbaugh in his message entitled *"Scratching Our Itches"* writes the following in his excellent discourse:

"Paul's description of people having 'itching ears' is picturesque. The Greek word, knethomai, literally means "to itch, rub, scratch, or tickle." This figure of speech implies that they have an itch that must be scratched, or as William Barclay puts it, "they have ears which have to be continually titillated with novelties'" (The Letters to Timothy, Titus, and Philemon, p. 202). "Such people open their ears to any teacher who will relieve their particular "itch" ***regardless of how it measures against the truth***.

The solution to this resides in proper discernment based on God's infallible Word. This judgment must be based on His whole counsel. John writes, 'Beloved, do not believe every spirit, but test the spirits, whether they are of God; because many false prophets have gone out into the world' (I John 4:1). Christ commends the Ephesian church for this: I know your works, your labor, your patience, and that you cannot bear those who are evil. And you have tested those who say they are apostles and are not, and have found them liars. (Revelation 2:2)   Paul says it most simply, 'Test all things; hold fast what is good' (I Thessalonians 5:21). It is our Christian duty to evaluate the "causes" we endorse. Are they truly of God, or are they itches we want scratched? Have we allowed the world to influence our thinking, or are we on solid biblical footing? Have we held our ground against Satan, or have we given in to his relentless onslaught?'"

In conclusion, despite fair Mormon's defense of the burning in the bosom test, Mormon leaders know the evidence is not there. In knowing this, they created a *"highly subjective"* standard that completely bypasses looking at or examining any evidence, in fact as we already read and as a few youtube videos show, if you search they strongly discourage it knowing that it may very well result in one losing their faith in the LDS Church. Which is precisely why the LDS Church is presently losing more members than ever before. In this *"age of information"* where fact checking is only a few clicks away on the computer, one can now have the information at their fingertips in a matter of minutes. Unlike those in times past who did not have that necessity. So we've seen the Bible clearly teaches *"blind* faith" is neither biblical nor wise. 1st John 4:1 states it best: *Dear friends, do not believe every spirit, but **test the spirits** to determine if they are from God, because many **false prophets** have gone out into the world.* So John tells us to TEST the spirits, not to just merely believe whatever they say! Another passage that is disturbing is found in the last verse of John's account of the Gospel in verse 41 where Jesus, in speaking to the Pharisees stated this: *"If you were blind," Jesus told them, "you wouldn't have sin. But now that you say, 'We see'—your sin remains.* This sadly refers to those Mormons who know the truth and yet continue to deny it, to them Jesus says: *But now that you say, 'We see' -- your sin remains"*.

Denying facts and placing our heads in the sand like an Ostrich, only serves to further bolster the argument of those who sarcastically claim that Religion or Faith of any kind requires one to *"check their brain at the door."* Sadly, LDS followers are near the top of that list for some of the reasons I have already pointed out and will continue to do so throughout this book. In the next chapter, we will seek to answer the question: *"Is the Mormon Church in decline?"*

Chapter Seven

Is The Mormon Church In Decline?

Quite a provocative title for a chapter is it not? The question before us is whether or not it's true. Let's see if we can answer that question in this chapter. Here is a little bit of a dialogue that took place on a podcast between Dr. William Lane Craig and host Kevin Harris. The podcast was entitled *"Is Mormonism in Decline?"*

"Some reports say Mormons are leaving their church in record numbers. But Dr. Craig gets to the heart of the matter"

Kevin Harris: *"Dr. Craig, our Mormon friends would probably be very interested in today's podcast. Many Mormons would be aware that there are reports that Mormons are leaving the LDS Church in record numbers. Let's talk a little bit about this today. We're looking at a blog from Defend magazine. James Walker, who is president of Watchman Fellowship, has done a lot of research on Mormonism. He is studying why there are these reports that there really is a trend of Mormons leaving the LDS Church. He quotes Reuters and he does his research here. Why are Mormons leaving the church 'in droves?' The surprising question was posed to Elder Marlin K. Jensen, church historian and recorder for the Church of Jesus Christ of Latter-day Saints. The answer may be equally surprising. James K. Walker, president of Watchman Fellowship, an independent Christian research and apologetics ministry focusing on new religious movements . . . addressed the question of why Mormons disbelieve. While the Church of Jesus Christ of Latter-day Saints, (LDS) took 117 years from its founding to reach its first 1 million members, growth in the 20th century and beyond is said to be closer to one million added worldwide every three years, Walker said. In the 1980s, author and historian Rodney Stark predicted that the LDS church could reach world religion status if the growth rate continued"*

Then something changed.

"Something went very badly wrong on the road to world domination," Walker said. A Jan. 31, 2012 Reuters special report, *"Mormonism besieged by the modern age,"* reported on Jensen's unscripted, candid remarks to the question posed above that were recorded while speaking at a small gathering at Utah State

University. Reporters Peter Henderson and Kristina Cooke wrote this: *"Did the leaders of the Church of Jesus Christ of Latter-Day Saints know that members are leaving in droves a woman asked" "We are aware,"* said Jensen, according to a tape recording of his unscripted remarks. *"And I'm speaking of the 15 men that are above me in the hierarchy of the church. They really do know, and they really care,"* he said. *"My own daughter,"* he then added, *"has come to me and said, Dad, why didn't you tell me that Joseph Smith was a polygamist?'"*

The reporters noted the rising tide of questions from church members about issues regarding the Book of Mormon and the historical problems that have been largely glossed over by Mormon leaders. Walker pointed out that Jensen placed blame on the internet. The article reported this: *"for the younger generation, Jensen acknowledged, everything's out there for them to consume if they want to Google it.'"*

The article goes on to say:

"Bill, I tell you, there are so many things on Mormonism and on all religions and worldviews; if you want to research it you'll get it. But what is very embarrassing to many

Mormons is that things that are very sacred to them and have always been done very secretively are now all over YouTube. Like the baptismal ceremonies that they do for the dead. The Mormon marriages and the garb that they wear referred to as Mormon underwear and all such things. People have sneaked in cell phones and video cams. Now it is just splashed all over YouTube. A lot of people go, "Boy that is strange." So, in one sense the Internet may be responsible for some things, but one can only speculate why Mormons are leaving the church. End of podcast excerpt.

Now in all fairness, Dr. Lane goes on to say it could also be part of the overall downturn in general toward Religion in our Society, to that there is no question I think for the most part. I have watched many of those YouTube videos, especially the ones that were recorded secretly inside Mormon Temples. To Biblical Christians, they are *"strange"* to say the least, highly unusual garb, secret masonic type handshakes and the like, all being done to gain access to God repeatedly despite Biblical passages like *Ephesians 2:8-9* and *Titus 3:5-6* which make it clear that it's impossible for us to in any way, shape, or form to earn or work our way into heaven. It's really heart breaking to see how hard so many Mormons work as well as how many hours they spend thinking via this route they will inherit eternal life. For true believers know salvation has already been freely made available and without any cost of work or labor on our part, Christ did it all. Now works will follow…… Biblical works that is, as they are a **byproduct** of true belief, but they cannot bring about salvation in any way!

Jana Riess, who calls herself a *"progressive Mormon,"* is starting to look at millennials in the LDS church. She quotes numbers from the Pew Research Center, showing a retention rate today *(2017)* of Mormon millennials at 64 percent, compared to the 1970s and '80s when retention was at roughly 90 percent for born-and-raised Mormons. Riess, the author of *"Flunking Sainthood,"* is a senior columnist for Religion News Service and spoke on a recent panel at Utah Valley University. She spoke of change within the LDS church, to which she belongs:

"Many of the values the millennial generation has stated are inclusion, tolerance and are not values they feel are being reflected. Millennials are more supportive of social change, like gay marriage, than their parents and don't agree with some of the stances the LDS church has

taken in recent years" Let me make it clear here that the LDS Church has taken a stand against some of the social changes that have been *"blowing in the wind"* these past few years that do not reflect Biblical or Godly principles and they should be commended for that. Here is an article I found, albeit it is now close to 14 years old, but none-the-less very informative:

In John L. Smith's latest Newsletter *(Nov-Dec 2003),* he published the following statistics about the number of Mormons who are requesting name removal. He said his source was from *"someone inside the church."* They represent the years of 1995 through 2002.

For what they are worth, here they are:

1995: 35,420

1996: 50,177

1997: 55,200

1998: 78,750

1999: 81,200

2000: 87,500

2001: 101,454

2002: 105,763

If these numbers are reliable, then the number of Mormons requesting name removal has **tripled** in seven years.

Thus, I think it's fair to say the Mormon claim to being the *"fastest-growing church" (in America, or in the world, or whatever)* should be corrected as the *"fastest-shrinking church."* Or perhaps, the Ex-Mormons are the *"fastest-growing non-church."* Interestingly, the Mormon Church tries to keep these statistics from the public.

Here are a few important current graphs to look at. My thanks to the website: *RoundelMike.com* for these figures.

Please note these figures come from the LDS church itself. They self-report their numbers, and there's no way to verify anything. Still, I have no reason to believe that the Mormon Church is not being truthful about their statistics.

First, let's have a look at total LDS church membership, by year.

Mormon Church Membership

In 2016, the Mormon Church grew to 15,882,417 members, which is about what we should expect, considering the trend since 1970. People sometimes say the LDS church is growing exponentially, but the numbers show it's not. Instead, the growth is quite linear, especially since about 1990. Yearly membership is predictable. There aren't any peaks or valleys in this chart, and growth is steady. For more information, let's have a look at year-over-year figures:

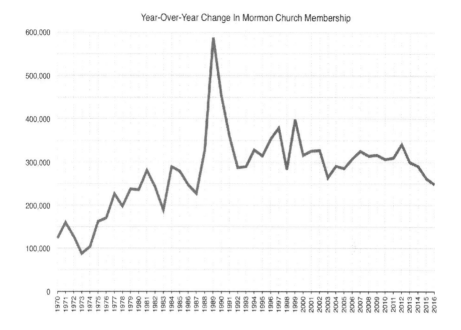

Year-Over-Year Change In Mormon Church Membership

This graph shows year-over-year growth for each year, and it's simple to calculate. From the previous graph, we know how many members the Mormon Church has each year. To calculate the change in membership, we subtract the membership for each year from the preceding year. This figure isn't specific about how these members are added; it's simply a year over year change. Since 1992, there have been roughly 315,000 members added each year. The past four years have been down years. The year 2016 was low, at 248,218, which is the fewest since 1987.

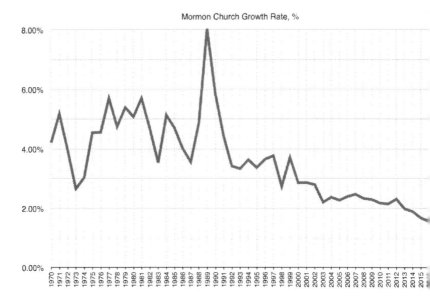

Mormon Church Growth Rate, %

And we will see the clear evidence of decline in the final graph coming up on page 87.

This graph is calculated by dividing each year's change in membership by total membership for each year. In 2013, the growth rate dropped below 2% for the first time, and it has gone down since, with 2016 at 1.56%. The growth rate is erratic, especially before 2000. But it has steadily declined overall since 1970. Put simply, a smaller percentage of Mormons are new members than ever before. Like any other organization, it's easier to have large growth rates when things are small. Now that the Mormon Church is large, it's harder to add ever-increasing numbers of people.

To look at one component of that growth, we can examine convert baptisms.

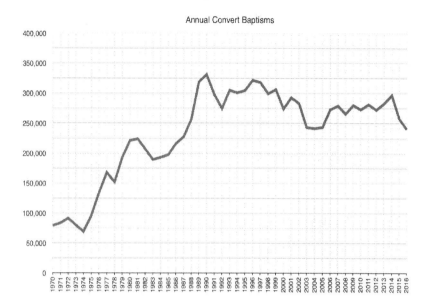

Annual Convert Baptisms

The evidence suggests the Mormon Church has been in decline since roughly 1989-90, around the same time the internet really began to take off, coincidence?

It seems to me the evidence is obvious. The correlation between the internet taking off and the LDS Church's decline in membership from prior years is clearly due in large part to the Web. Many people now have access to needed information and they are capable of making an informed decision unlike in times past. Clearly in times past, *(prior to 89-90)* individuals had a much harder time finding the needed sources to verify LDS claims. Another example relevant to this conversation is that the LDS Church is experiencing good growth in Africa to this day. Is it any coincidence where this growth is taking place is due to the fact many of the countries there have little to no access to the internet?

The facts included here via the graphs speak for themselves: the Mormon Church is indeed experiencing steadily declining numbers. When such an insider in the hierarchy of the Mormon Church such as Marlin K. Jensen can acknowledge such, then you take that to the bank so to speak. This is because LDS leaders have always been very *"tightlipped"* about admitting such things in the past. Thus, it has become painfully obvious they can no longer continue to lose the numbers they have and hide them. When articles like this one in the Salt Lake Tribune report the following, it becomes clear that they can't manipulate the numbers anymore. An April 15, 2016 report says the Mormon millennials retention rate has dipped to an all-time low of 64% vs. roughly 90% thirty plus years ago. The bottom line is the Church is now losing roughly 36% of its members, a staggering number! *(This is the same article where Jana Riess got her numbers that were listed earlier on pages 105-6 as they are exact!)* In closing, I have taken notice of the stories I have heard of Mormons who left after making their 1st visit to the Temple. From the feedback I have gotten, they were actually frightened or were very confused about all the *"secret"* rituals that went on at the Temple and were left to wonder how they could possibly be related to Biblical Christianity? Some of the stories are quite eerie as many felt uneasy and the sense of *"spirits"* of unknown origin during the ceremonies which was disconcerting to them.

I will say this, when one examines the connection between Joseph Smith and Freemasonry, after being forced out of Ohio and Missouri to later in 1840 begin the town of Nauvoo, Illinois. His forming a Masonic Lodge with many of the early members of the LDS Church who were already Masons such as: Brigham Young, Heber C. Kimball, John C. Bennett, Hyrum Smith and Joseph Smith, Sr. among others. It's no coincidence that in 1842 after Joseph Smith's joining into Freemasonry that these secretive ceremonies like the temple endowment ceremony and much of the symbolism used in such ceremonies closely mirrored Masonic practice. I will not write much on this topic, but I can tell you that there is a lot of information linking many Mormon ceremonies to Masonic practices and symbolism. For instance, it is known that the *"garment"* Mormons wear contains symbols of Freemasonry—the Square, Compass, and Rule. Again, there is a lot of information on the web about LDS practices and its close ties to Freemasonry. *(which would certainly help to explain the uneasiness of many who left after going through the Temple rituals and ceremonies feeling a "dark" presence for there is a direct link between Freemasonry and Occult practices, see link below on this page)* There is also a wealth of books on the subject. One bit of information in particular I would highly recommend is this powerful article from Sandra Tanner at:

http://www.utlm.org/onlineresources/masonics ymbolsandtheldstemple.htm

Occult and Freemasonry Link:

https://www.jashow.org/articles/guests-and-authors/dave-hunt/the-occult-influence-in-freemasonry/

Chapter Eight

Did The Gospel Need To Be Restored?

One of the most important doctrines that Mormonism espouses is the idea they are the *"restored church of Jesus Christ on the earth today"* They push this heavily, and their missionaries share day after day in the field across the globe. *(Totaling at any time some 50,000 young men and women sharing the Mormon gospel)* Mormons believe that somehow over the many Centuries the Bible and the Gospel of Jesus Christ became corrupted and even partially lost. One of the Mormon articles of faith, number 8, states: *"We believe the Bible to be the word of God, as far as it is translated correctly"* Of course, it goes without saying since the LDS Church clearly states it is the restoration of the Christian Church, then who would be the only holders of the correct translation of the Bible?

You guessed it: The LDS Church and no one else. The truth is any committed and knowledgeable Mormon looks at the Bible skeptically. And since the Bible contradicts the Book of Mormon as well as Doctrines and

Covenants (D&C) as we have already proven in so many places, they had to add that spiritual "*caveat*". And as I showed earlier in chapter 3, the Book of Mormon and D&C also contradict each other in many places. Okay, let's look at the claim from 1st Nephi chapter 13:1-12 where this well thought out idea of a restoration of the Church was needed. Then we will take a short look at the evidence. I say short because I could write a thousand pages easily on the avalanche of evidence contrary to *this empty claim.*

1st Nephi 13:1-12: "And it came to pass that the angel spake unto me, saying: Look! And I looked and beheld many nations and kingdoms. And the angel said unto me: What beholdest thou? And I said: I behold many nations and kingdoms. And he said unto me: These are the nations and kingdoms of the Gentiles. And it came to pass that I saw among the nations of the Gentiles the formation of a great church. And the angel said unto me: Behold the formation of a church which is most abominable above all other churches, which slayeth the saints of God, yea, and tortureth them and bindeth them down, and yoketh them with a yoke of iron, and bringeth them down into captivity. And it came to pass that I beheld this great and abominable church; and

I saw the devil that he was the founder of it. And I also saw gold, and silver, and silks, and scarlets, and fine twined linen, and all manner of precious clothing; and I saw many harlots. And the angel spake unto me, saying: Behold the gold, and the silver, and the silks, and the scarlets, and the fine-twined linen, and the precious clothing, and the harlots, are the desires of this great and abominable church. And also for the praise of the world do they destroy the saints of God, and bring them down into captivity. And it came to pass that I looked and beheld many waters; and they divided the Gentiles from the seed of my brethren. And it came to pass that the angel said unto me: Behold the wrath of God is upon the seed of thy brethren. And I looked and beheld a man among the Gentiles, who was separated from the seed of my brethren by the many waters; and I beheld the Spirit of God, that it came down and wrought upon the man; and he went forth upon the many waters, even unto the seed of my brethren, who were in the promised land. In these first twelve verses, we see the case being made that a restoration was needed, shortly we will see the "why" In this portion thus far we've read what the Church will do; slayeth the saints of God, yea, and tortureth them and bindeth them down, and yoketh them with a yoke of iron, and bringeth them down into captivity. As well as the desires of this great and abominable church. And also for the praise of the world do they destroy the saints of God, and bring them down into captivity." In this next section, we will see the why, 1st Nephi chapter 13:20-28; 20: "And it came to pass that I, Nephi, beheld that they did prosper in the land; and I beheld a book, and it was carried forth among them. And the angel said unto me: Knowest thou the meaning of the book? And I said unto him: I know not. And he said: Behold it proceedeth out of the mouth of a Jew. And I, Nephi, beheld it; and he said unto me: The book that thou beholdest is a record of the Jews, which contains the covenants of the Lord, which he hath made unto the house of Israel; and it also containeth many of the prophecies of the holy prophets; and it is a record like unto the engravings which are upon the plates of brass, save there are not so many; nevertheless, they contain the covenants of the Lord, which he hath made unto the house of Israel; wherefore, they are of great worth unto the Gentiles. And the angel of the Lord said unto me: Thou hast beheld that the book proceeded forth from the mouth of a Jew; and when it proceeded forth from the mouth of a Jew it contained the fulness (sic) of the gospel of the Lord, of whom the twelve apostles bear record;

and they bear record according to the truth which is in the Lamb of God. Wherefore, these things go forth from the Jews in purity unto the Gentiles, according to the truth which is in God. And after they go forth by the hand of the twelve apostles of the Lamb, from the Jews unto the Gentiles, thou seest the formation of that great and abominable church, which is most abominable above all other churches; for behold, they have taken away from the gospel of the Lamb many parts which are plain and most precious; and also many covenants of the Lord have they taken away. And all this have they done that they might pervert the right ways of the Lord that they might blind the eyes and harden the hearts of the children of men. Wherefore, thou seest that after the book hath gone forth through the hands of the great and abominable church, that there are many plain and a precious thing taken away from the book, which is the book of the Lamb of God.

As I previously stated, here we see the why. So now one must ask the question: Are these things true and can these claims be verified? I'm afraid many of our Mormon friends may say something to the effect of, *"Just pray about them, and don't bother yourself with whether or not there is evidence."* I say this based on what they are being told by their leaders as we have already read. Go to this YouTube video link to hear Mormon Elder M. Russell Ballard literally say what I just stated. Please watch and listen for yourself: (https://www.youtube.com/watch?v=Qv3Udvc I21k)

He shares at a LDS youth meeting that LDS people should *"not get caught up in researching any claims."* He says to just stay in the teachings of the Church and the Book of Mormon. As a Pastor, I find that statement incredibly frightening and controlling. I could never in good conscience or otherwise stand before my people and say, *"Friends, you have my teachings, so you have no reason to research anything outside of what I say"* I'm sorry to say, but that is *"cultish"* talk. It controls people's minds, and I have seen it countless times in my dealings with faithful, well-meaning Mormons. I like a quote I used earlier from J. Rueben Clark: ***"If we have the truth, it cannot be harmed by investigation. If we have not the truth, it ought to be harmed."***

Now, let's continue to examine these claims made in 1st Nephi. Here, we will look at the first set of claims made in chapter 13 of 1st Nephi, verses 1-12.

Is there any evidence of a latter-day church that persecuted the saints of God and took them into captivity? What's also interesting is I hear language in these verses that seem to be borrowed from the Book of Revelation including, the talk of a harlot and of the saints being slain. To be honest, there wasn't much I could find. There was a Captivity of Mangalorean Catholics at Seringapatam (1784–1799). This was a 15-year imprisonment of Mangalorean Catholics and other Christians at Seringapatam in the Indian region of Canara by Tipu Sultan, the de facto ruler of the Kingdom of Mysore. Estimates of the number of captives range from 30,000 to 80,000 but the generally accepted figure is 60,000, as stated by Tipu in the Sultan-ul-Tawarikh. The captivity was the most disconsolate period in the community's history. Its cause is disputed however, it is generally agreed by historians it was purely due to religious reasons.

And those who know their Church history know the Catholic Church persecuted believers who didn't accept the papacy. Foxes book of Martyrs in Chapter IV describes many of the various persecutions and starts the chapter by saying the following: *"We come now to a period when persecution, under the guise of*

Christianity, committed more enormities than ever disgraced the annals of paganism. Disregarding the maxims and the spirit of the Gospel, the papal Church, arming herself with the power of the sword, vexed the Church of God and wasted it for several centuries, a period most appropriately termed in history, the "dark ages." The kings of the earth, gave their power to the Beast, and submitted to be trodden on by the miserable vermin that often filled the papal chair, as in the case of Henry, emperor of Germany. The storm of papal persecution first burst upon the Waldenses in France. By the year of Christ 1140, the number of the reformed was very great, and the probability of its increasing alarmed the pope, who wrote to several princes to banish them from their dominions, and employed many learned men to write against their doctrines"

In A.D. 1147, because of Henry of Toulouse, deemed their most eminent preacher, they were called Henericians; and as they would not admit of any proofs relative to religion, but what could be deduced from the Scriptures themselves, the popish party gave them the name of apostolics. At length, Peter Waldo, or Valdo, a native of Lyons, eminent for his piety and learning, became a strenuous opposer of popery; and from him the reformed, at that time, received the appellation of Waldenses or Waldoys. Pope Alexander III being informed by the bishop of Lyons of these transactions, excommunicated Waldo and his adherents, and commanded the bishop to exterminate them, if possible, from the face of the earth; hence began the papal persecutions against the Waldenses. The proceedings of Waldo and the reformed, occasioned the first rise of the inquisitors; for Pope Innocent III authorized certain monks as inquisitors, to inquire for, and deliver over, the reformed to the secular power. The process was short, as an accusation was deemed adequate to guilt, and a candid trial was never granted to the accused. The pope, finding that these cruel means had not the intended effect, sent several learned monks to preach among the Waldenses, and to endeavor to argue them out of their opinions. Among these monks was one Dominic, who appeared extremely zealous in the cause of popery. This Dominic instituted an order, which, from him, was called the order of Dominican friars; and the members of this order have ever since been the principal inquisitors in the various inquisitions in the world. The power of the inquisitors was unlimited; they proceeded against whom they pleased, without any consideration of age, sex, or rank. Let the accusers be ever so infamous, the accusation was deemed valid; and even anonymous information's, sent by letter, were thought sufficient evidence. To be rich was a crime equal to heresy; therefore, many who had money were accused of heresy, or of being favorers of heretics, that they might be obliged to pay for their opinions."

The chapter then goes on for many more pages. Now it is true that the Catholic Church did indeed *"wear out or persecute"* the saints of God for a period, but nowhere on the scale recorded by the BOM! So now notice the language beginning in verse 12 of 1 Nephi 13: *"And I looked and beheld a man among the Gentiles, who was separated from the seed of my brethren by the many waters; and I beheld the Spirit of God, that it came down and wrought upon the man; and he went forth upon the many waters, even unto the seed of my brethren, who were in the promised land."* I wonder who this gentile man might be? Of course to the Mormon, this is a reference to the *"savior like"* figure, Joseph Smith. I hope you see this breakdown thus far. First, the rising up of an abominable and wicked Church which would obviously mean some kind of restoration would be needed. Then here comes the man who will be the *"Prophet"* or

"Overseer" of that needed restorative church. Are you getting the picture? However, there's more. Rather than looking again at the rise of this so called *"abominable Church"* which history doesn't record, let's look at more of the *"why"* a restoration and even extra biblical revelation, *(one of the first signs of a Cult, the Bible plus)* was needed.

Picking up in verse 26 of 1st Nephi 13 we read: *"And after they go forth by the hand of the twelve apostles of the Lamb, from the Jews unto the Gentiles, thou seest the formation of that great and abominable church, which is most abominable above all other churches; for behold, they have taken away from the gospel of the Lamb many parts which are plain and most precious; and also many covenants of the Lord have they taken away. And all this have they done that they might pervert the right ways of the Lord that they might blind the eyes and harden the hearts of the children of men. Wherefore, thou seest that after the book hath gone forth through the hands of the great and abominable church, that there are many plain and a precious thing taken away from the book, which is the book of the Lamb of God."*

This is an *"aha"* moment! A new revelation or revelations are needed because this abominable church took away various parts of the Scriptures *(the Bible).* Hence the LDS Church's 8th Article of Faith that we've already looked at! Now can you understand why a true LDS member always looks at the Bible with skepticism for its correctness despite its claim to be the very true divine Word of God: *(2 Tim. 3:16, 2 Pet. 1:20-21, John 17:17, Matt. 5:18, 1 Thess. 2:13, Heb. 6:18, Isa. 40:8, John 10:35, and Prov. 30:5 just to list a few).* Let's put this claim to the test as we did the last one. Is it true that parts of the Bible were corrupted or missing? Friends, of all the things Joseph Smith could have chosen to pick on; this was by far the worst. A Professor I know here in Lynchburg, Dr. Randall Price of Liberty University and the author of *"Searching for the Original Bible,"*

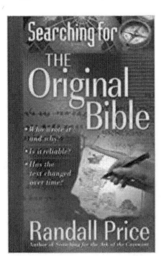

makes the validity of God's Word today crystal clear in his book. *(see pic on pg. 104)* Dr. Price's book is also substantiated by the Dead Sea Scrolls. Another great book that shows us God's Word has never suffered loss *(as God's Word clearly claims in the verses above)* is one headed by scholar and author, Norman Geisler entitled *"Inerrancy"* . *(see pic below)*

This is another in a series of books sponsored by the International Council on Biblical Inerrancy. The fourteen leading evangelical scholars who have contributed to this volume come from various denominations and have written on a wide range of topics related to the inerrancy of the Bible. Believing this doctrine is *"an essential element of the authority of Scripture and a necessary ingredient for the health of the church of Christ."* They have made a strong defense of it. As I said before, I could go on here, but you get the point. No such loss of Scripture over the centuries has ever happened friends. At last count my understanding is we have around 40,000 manuscripts/autographs so the claim in the BOM is undeniably false! Last, since a so called restoration was needed, then a man who would lead that restoration along with the LDS claims that the Bible was now corrupted; a new book or books of revelations would also be required! Let's start again in 1st Nephi chapter 13 and verse 20 to read about this new Book containing these *"so called lost revelations"*.

"And it came to pass that I, Nephi, beheld that they did prosper in the land; and I beheld a book, and it was carried forth among them. And the angel said unto me: Knowest thou the meaning of the book? And I said unto him: I know not. And he said: Behold it proceedeth out of the mouth of a Jew. And I, Nephi, beheld it; and he said unto me: The book that thou beholdest is a record of the Jews, which contains the covenants of the Lord, which he hath made unto the house of Israel; and it also containeth many of the prophecies of the holy prophets; and it is a record like unto the engravings which are upon the plates of brass, save there are not so many; nevertheless,

they contain the covenants of the Lord, which he hath made unto the house of Israel; wherefore, they are of great worth unto the Gentiles. And the angel of the Lord said unto me: Thou hast beheld that the book proceeded forth from the mouth of a Jew; and when it proceeded forth from the mouth of a Jew it contained the fulness (sic) of the gospel of the Lord, of whom the twelve apostles bear record; and they bear record according to the truth which is in the Lamb of God".

Any guesses what this *"latter day"* Scripture might be? You got it; the Book of Mormon which once accepted opens the door for the other so called revelations as well. So when one looks at the facts, these three unsubstantiated prophecies simply don't hold up. We can only conclude Nephi fails the test of a Biblical prophet as laid out for us in Deuteronomy 18:22: **"When a prophet speaks in the LORD's name, and the message does not come true or is not fulfilled, that is a message the LORD has not spoken. The prophet has spoken it presumptuously. Do not be afraid of him."** Both history and Scripture clearly testify against the BOM and Nephi's prophecy. As an important side note, this is also how the LDS Church can get away with the highly unusual

(I'm being nice) Temple rituals and endless works. When they mention terms like the *"covenants of the Lord"* or *"the fullness of the Gospel"*, these have far different meanings to Mormons, because they are pure works they must perform in order to hope to reach the *"highest"* heaven. In addition, the LDS Church has even perverted the biblical concept and teaching of Grace. To us who know Christ Jesus personally, Grace is a completely free gift. We can do nothing whatsoever to earn it. I earlier shared 2 important verses that are worth repeating here before we see the Mormon concept of grace. First is Ephesians 2:8-9: *"For you are saved by grace through faith, and this is not from yourselves; it is God's gift— 9 not from works, so that no one can boast."* And next is Titus 3:4-7: *"But when the goodness of God and His love for mankind appeared, 5 He saved us— not by works of righteousness that we had done, but according to His mercy, through the washing of regeneration and renewal by the Holy Spirit. 6 He poured out this [Spirit] on us abundantly through Jesus Christ our Savior, 7 so that having been justified by His grace; we may become heirs with the hope of eternal life."* The LDS Church in the following verse from the BOM has added to the biblical concept of Grace.

2nd Nephi 25:23 makes this incredibly unbiblical pronouncement: *"For we labor diligently to write, to persuade our children, and our brethren, to believe in Christ, and to be reconciled to God; for we know that it is by grace that we are saved, **after all we can do."** After all we can do? The Bible talks clearly about adding or taking away from God's Holy Word and this is certainly an example of that.

Additionally, Revelation 22:18-19: *I testify to everyone who hears the prophetic words of this book: If anyone adds to them, God will add to him the plagues that are written in this book. 19 And if anyone takes away from the words of this prophetic book, God will take away his share of the tree of life and the holy city, written in this book.*

Need I add anything further here?

Chapter Nine

How to Reach Mormons

In this chapter, I will share some of my thoughts as well as the thoughts of those who have far more experience than me. Since writing this chapter, I have had the opportunity to lead a family out of Mormonism. They renounced their membership, involvement, and baptism in the LDS Church. *(It's actually really simple thanks to a compassionate former member who is an Atty.in Salt Lake City, Mark A. Naugle. Just go to: quitmormon.com)* Thankfully by God's Grace this family has quickly made the transition to Biblical Christianity. Unfortunately, many people *(I'm told some 40%)* who come out of Pseudo Christian sects often do not come into that personal relationship with the Biblical God or His Son, Jesus Christ and that is very distressing indeed. How sad when one turns completely away from the Savior because of fraudulent religion. To anyone reading this book contemplating walking away altogether, please read Jesus' words closely and carefully in John 14:6, they are either true or false and I can personally attest, as can millions that they are

100% true! For this book let's call them *"Nick and Ann."* I met Nick online as I was looking through a few posts I knew were Mormon. After praying for a bit, I felt led to contact him. His response was almost immediate. I started my initial contact two ways. First, I identified myself and asked if he was willing to have *"honest and open dialogue"* on the history and doctrines of the LDS Church? Second, I sent him a link to what I believe is perhaps one of the most powerful short to the point testimonies from a former Mormon on the internet today. And that is Micah Wilder's testimony video of roughly 17 minutes. I prefaced it with this: *"Here is a video I would truly appreciate your feedback on, please".* Here is that link, and I strongly suggest you use it in your witnessing efforts to our LDS friends. But do so only after having watched it in its entirety first please!

Link to Micah's video: (https://www.youtube.com/watch?v=D569x5T qtVk)

Micah Wilder, the person in this video, who is also the founder of Adam's Road Ministry, writes the following: *"When the Mormon missionaries or Jehovah's Witnesses come to your door, don't reject them. Don't mock them. Don't ridicule them. Don't treat them unkindly. Love them. Have compassion on them. Show them respect, kindness, and gentleness. And most importantly, tell them about Jesus! Remember who we are and who we are called to be. We are called to love others as Christ has loved us, and in that love, we share the goodness and grace of God through Christ Jesus."* Here are a few thoughts on sharing with our Mormon friends I want to stress:

•   Don't engage in arguing!   Arguments never win anyone. Yes, you may win a few *"battles",* but you will undoubtedly lose the *"war for their soul"*

•   Be honest and be up front. What I mean by this is do not suddenly pull Jesus or a surprise out of your back pocket! People feel deceived when you do that, thus we should always be up front and honest about our motives. Since I am usually engaged in serious *"cold turkey"* outreach, I often get this question from my Mormon friends I am contacting: *"why are you contacting me, what's your angle here?"* My response is honest, clear and concise: *"it's because I love Mormon people and have a real heart to share truth with them"* When they hear that, 80% of the time a good conversation begins!

•   Do not bash or ridicule them or the LDS Church. Oh yes, point out error by all means, but do it in a way that shows true and heartfelt respect. I have found that many of the Mormons I talk to truly appreciate this approach which results in longer engagements which will over time, as the Holy Spirit works on their hearts yield fruit as they will not be able to forget what you are saying to them. This leads me to another important point

•   Be patient! As I stated in an earlier chapter, building bridges takes time, so start with things that are not so *"heavy"* and then work your way to stronger issues because as the bridge to that person gets stronger, the more *"weight"* you can begin to navigate across it. Sometimes it takes years friends!

•   As much as you can, use Mormon literature when possible. It has a much more lasting and powerful effect when you show a Mormon their own quotes, false prophecies and wayward unorthodox doctrines. This shows them you are not trying to bash them or have an *"axe to grind"* so to speak.

• Last, this is serious business; don't play with people's hearts and minds. I am forever cognizant of the fact that I can be in a sense *"dismantling"* someone's hopes and dreams. I take that to heart very seriously which is why I mentioned earlier that when I share with my Congregation about outreach, I tell them that they have a huge responsibility if they are going to share Jesus with someone and not to attempt to do so unless they are fully willing to invest into that person and their life! The same applies here friends. Don't help a person out of the maze of Mormonism unless you are willing to love them, help them, spend time with them and ultimately help them lay their feet and life on the firm foundation of the Word of God and Jesus Christ! Take time to think of when you and I were searching. Think of those loving and caring brothers and sisters who came alongside us and nurtured and navigated us through the early *"minefields"* we were walking through. Thus, do likewise to our Mormon friends here who will have plenty of their own minefields to navigate in these precious early days and years.

Chapter Ten

Why Mormonism Is Not Christian

There are very good and solid reasons why Mormonism cannot be considered an Orthodox Christian Faith. In this chapter we will investigate exactly why. Mormonism, via the teachings of both Joseph Smith and Brigham Young, which have been carried on through to today, have steadfastly been in denial of Biblical, Historic Orthodox Christian doctrine. Let's look at a few of the most blatant denials of Biblical, Historic Orthodoxy by Mormonism.

The Virgin Birth of Jesus Christ

The Bible is clear that Jesus was born of a virgin, a woman who had not had ANY physical/sexual relationship with a man.

*Matthew 1:23: See, the **virgin** will become pregnant and give birth to a son, and they will name Him Immanuel, which is translated "God is with us."* The word Virgin in Greek is: *"Parthenos"* It is used 14 times in the N.T. and means *"a maiden, an unmarried woman"*.

*Luke 1:26-27: In the sixth month, the angel Gabriel was sent by God to a town in Galilee called Nazareth, 27 to a **virgin** engaged to a* man named Joseph, of the house of David. The virgin's name was Mary. The O.T. also substantiates that Mary was a virgin as we read this:

Isaiah 7:14: *Therefore, the Lord Himself will give you a sign: The **virgin** will conceive, have a son, and name him Immanuel.*

Mormonism teaches the following:

The late Mormon Apostle Bruce R. McConkie, in perhaps the most explicit denial of the virgin birth wrote, *"Christ was begotten by an immortal Father in the **same way** that mortal men are begotten by mortal fathers." (Mormon Doctrine, 1966, p. 547)* You might ask, *"How can Mormons who believe this say that Christ was born of a virgin?"* This is done by changing the definition of the word *"virgin".* The virgin Mary did not have sexual relations with a mortal man, they say, but instead was impregnated by an immortal man. Bruce R. McConkie wrote, *"Our Lord is the only mortal person ever born to a virgin, because he is the only person who ever had an immortal Father." (Mormon Doctrine, 2nd ed., p. 822)*

2nd LDS President Brigham Young stated this: *"The Father came down and begat him, **the same as we do now**..." (The Complete*

Discourses of Brigham Young, vol. 1, p. 321; February 16, 1849, Salt Lake City) Ezra Taft Benson, former LDS President: *"I am bold to say to you... The Church of Jesus Christ of Latter-day Saints proclaims that Jesus Christ is the Son of God in the most literal sense. The body in which He performed His mission in the flesh was sired by that same Holy Being we worship as God, our Eternal Father. **Jesus was not the son of Joseph, nor was He begotten by the Holy Ghost**"* (The Teachings of Ezra Taft Benson, p. 7; cf. Come unto Christ, p. 4; cf. "Five Marks of the Divinity of Jesus Christ", Ensign, Dec. 2001, 8).

This is a direct denial of Luke's account given in Luke 1:35: *The angel replied to her: "The Holy Spirit will come upon you, and the **power of the Most High will overshadow you.** Therefore, the holy One to be born will be called the Son of God.* Webster's defines overshadowed as: *"to cover with a superior influence".* The Greek word here is: *"episkiasei"* which means to envelop in a haze of brilliancy. So there can be no question that Mormonism up to today denies the literal, actual virgin birth of Jesus Christ.

The Nature of the Biblical God

The one God is a Spirit who is the personal, eternal, infinite Creator of all that exists. He is the only God and necessary for all other things to exist. He exists eternally as a Trinity or Triune: Father, Son, and Holy Spirit. *(see Deut. 6:4; Isa. 43:10; 44:6-8; Matt. 28:19; John 4:24; 17:3)*

Mormonism on the Nature of God

God (Heavenly Father) is an **exalted man** with a **physical body of flesh and bone**. LDS founder Joseph Smith said, "If the veil were rent today, and the great God who holds this world in its orbit, and who upholds all worlds and all things by his power, was to make himself visible-I say, if you were to see him today, you would see him **like a man** in form" *(Teachings of the Prophet Joseph Smith, p. 345).*

Mormonism also denies another biblical, historic orthodox doctrine, *"The Trinity or Tri-unity"* of God. In Mormonism, the trinity is denied with the Father, the Son, and the Holy Ghost seen as three separate entities **among thousands of gods.** *"The Father has a body of flesh and bones as tangible as man's; the Son also; but the Holy Ghost has not a body of* *flesh and bones, but is a personage of Spirit. Were it not so, the Holy Ghost could not dwell in us" (Doctrine and Covenants [D&C] 130:22).*

Historic Authoritative Canon

The Bible *(Old and New Testaments)* is the unique, revealed, and inspired Word of God. It is the sole authority for faith and practice for Christians. *(see 2 Tim. 3:15-17; 2 Pet. 1:19-21)*

Mormonism: Recognizes the LDS four standard works as authoritative. These include the Bible *"as far as it is translated correctly" (Articles of Faith 1:8).* It also includes The Book of Mormon (BOM) which Joseph Smith declared is *"the most correct of any book on earth, and the keystone of our religion, and a man would get nearer to God by abiding by its precepts, than by **any other book**" (Teachings of the Prophet Joseph Smith, p. 194).* The church also regards The Doctrine and Covenants *(D&C)* as Scripture. It *"is a collection of modern revelations . . . regarding The Church of Jesus Christ as it has been restored in these last days" (GP, p. 54).* The Pearl of the Great Price *(PGP)* is the 3rd book believed to be inspired. *"It clarifies doctrines and teachings that were lost from the Bible and gives added* *information concerning the creation of the earth" (GP, p. 54).*

The Book of Abraham is the 4th *"authoritative"* book recognized that I spoke about early on pages 73-74 & the church's president is regarded as *"a seer, a revelator, a translator, and a prophet" (D&C 107:91-92).*

The Nature of Humanity

Human beings are created in God's image, meaning they have personal qualities similar to God's. Every person is a unique, precious being of dignity and worth. *(see Gen. 1:26-27)*

Mormonism: People are the preexisted spiritual offspring of the Heavenly Father and Mother. *"All men and women are . . . literally the sons and daughters of Deity . . . Man, as a spirit, was begotten and born of heavenly parents, and reared to maturity in the eternal mansions of the Father, prior to coming upon the earth in a temporal (physical) body" (Joseph F. Smith, "The Origin of Man," Improvement Era, Nov. 1909, pp. 78,80, as quoted in GP, p. 11).* They are born basically **good and are "gods in embryo."** A commonly quoted Mormon aphorism *(attributed to fifth LDS president Lorenzo Snow)* says **"As man is, God once was; as God is, man may become."**

How ironic and sad is it that Mormonism plays right into Satan's lie that tempted Adam and Eve with the notion that they can *"be like god?"* Gen. 3:5: *In fact, God knows that when you eat it your eyes will be opened and **you will be like God**, knowing good and evil."*

The Doctrine of Sin

Human beings have chosen to sin against God, rejecting His nature and pursing life opposed to His essential character and revealed law. *(see Rom. 3:23; 7:14-25; 1 John 1:8-10)*

Mormonism states: People sin by disobedience to God's laws. **Adam's fall, a part of Heavenly Father's plan**, caused a loss of immortality, which was **necessary** for mankind to advance, *(see GP, pp. 31-34).* As Eve declared according to LDS scripture, *"Were it not for our transgression we never should have . . . known good and evil, and the joy of our redemption, and the eternal life which God giveth unto all the obedient"(PGP, Moses 5:11; see also BOM, 2 Nephi 2:22-25).* Each person is responsible for his or her own sin. Yes, Mormonism teaches that sin actually brought joy! 2nd Nephi 2:25 incredibly states in utter contradiction to the Holy Bible: ***Adam fell that men might be; and men are, that they might have joy.***

The Doctrine of Salvation

Salvation is release from the guilt and power of sin through God's gift of grace. It is provided through Christ's atonement and received by personal faith in Christ as Savior and Lord and that not of ourselves, in other words, we cannot earn it. *(see Rom. 3:20; 10:9- 10; Eph. 2:8-10, Titus 3:5-6)*

Mormonism: Jesus' atonement provided immortality for all people. Exaltation *(godhood)* is available only to Mormons through obedience to LDS teachings: faith, baptism, endowments, celestial marriage, and tithing. *"Wherefore, as it is written, they are gods, even the sons of God-Wherefore, all things are theirs" (D&C, 76:58-59).* Thus, LDS teaching on salvation has added to God's Holy Word by the following: 2nd Nephi 2:23 *For we labor diligently to write, to persuade our children, and also our brethren, to believe in Christ, and to be reconciled to God; for we know that it is by grace that we are saved, **after all we can do.***

So from the evidence we have just read, it is crystal clear that Mormon doctrine is in direct and utter conflict with Biblical, Historic Orthodox Christianity. And because it is, when a person joins themselves to the LDS Church, they are clearly placing themselves **in danger of forfeiting the great gift of eternal life that God has offers us in Jesus Christ**. LDS or those considering joining the LDS Church would do well to heed the Apostle Paul's warning found in. Galatians 1:7-9: *not that there is another [gospel], but there are some who are troubling you and want to change the good news about the Messiah. 8 But even if we or an **angel from heaven** should preach to you a gospel other than what we have preached to you, **a curse be on him!** 9 As we have said before, I now say again: If anyone preaches to you a gospel contrary to what you received, **a curse be on him!***

This research makes it clear and incontrovertible that Mormonism is in direct conflict with Biblical, Historic, Orthodox Christian doctrine as handed down from God Almighty, through His Holy Word and Son right through the Apostles up to us today.

Chapter Eleven

Final Thoughts

Well a lot has been said already, but I'd like to share a few more things here. I want to emphasize that I LOVE LDS people and I believe a huge part of showing Biblical/Agape love is by being willing to *"place yourself out there once you've counted the cost, as Jesus taught" (Luke 14:28)* After all, didn't Jesus put Himself out there for us? Isn't that what our Heavenly Father did for us as well when He sent us His one and only Son? There is a wonderful, powerful statement that I read from a Watchtower *(Jehovah's Witnesses)* publication *(of all places!)* that I agree with 100%. It's from: *The Truth That Leads to Eternal Life, 1968 ed., p. 13*

"We need to examine, not only what we personally believe, but also what is taught by any religious organization with which we may be associated. Are its teachings in full harmony with God's Word, or are they based on the traditions of men? If we are lovers of the truth, there is nothing to fear from such an examination."

Was there ever a truer statement in regards to examining the teachings of the organization you are considering affiliation with than this? The problem I have found over and over again, which I actually experienced on the day of this writing in talking with a young Mormon lady is that so many Mormon converts have just *"jumped in feet first"* without fully examining the background, history and doctrines of the LDS Church only to realize later that something isn't quite right. And I would hold many Mormon Missionaries responsible for not sharing the *"fullness"* of what they know as I am totally convinced many of them know the problems with Mormon Theology and evidence. In most cases what has happened is that you may have trusted the presenter or missionaries who came to your door, perhaps it was a boyfriend or girlfriend that you wanted to get serious with who told you they can only go forward if you become LDS? To those who are reading this book who are in that early or late process of affiliation with the LDS Church, please do your *"do diligence"* **NOW!** Affiliating with a Pseudo *(counterfeit)* Christian organization is to put your very salvation on the line, one cannot and will not be able to claim ignorance before the throne of Almighty God when you had the evidence right here all along in front of you. Remember the verse from John 9:41 I shared on page 78? Jesus told those Pharisee's that because they claimed to see, that they would be held accountable and when a Mormon likewise claims to be right in the face of such an *"avalanche"* of evidence, I'd have to safely assume that the same fate would await such a person as well sadly…..

I promise you it will save you and your family and those to come in your family from much heartache, inner turmoil and pain for years! Believe me when I say that please. May my God help you in your journey as you seek to know and serve this Biblical God who sent His **only one of a kind** *(there are not thousands of gods out there, just one!)* Son into this world that *"whosoever should believe in Him, should not perish, but have everlasting life"*, Amen.

Chapter Twelve

Thanks and Endorsements

First off, I want to thank my wife, Dawn. Without her love, support and understanding of the time it takes to do such a labor of love, this book would never have come to light. Thank you for simply being you!

Special thanks also goes to Dr. Lynn Wilder whose testimony moved me to my core to again reach out and love my Mormon friends. I do this by telling them the truth as straight forward and as honest as possible while doing so in love as the Scripture teaches us to do to ALL people.

Another special thanks to the ministry of Adam's Road. *(www.adamsroadministry.com)*

This is one of the finest ministries around today as far as presenting the Gospel of Jesus Christ goes. These former Mormon missionaries are also gifted musicians and travel the country every year so be sure to look them up.

I want to thank Dr. Joe Stowell, President of Cornerstone University and the ultimate *"Pastor's Pastor"*. Your ministry has been such an encouragement to me and I just want to say thanks as God used you to lift me out of a deep dark time in my life many years ago, for that I will be forever grateful to your work and ministry.

Last, a special thanks to a dear brother in Christ who recently went home to be with the Lord, Elder Bruce Weaver. I had the pleasure of serving as his pastor for almost 8 years. Bruce and Marion, his dear wife who departed us a few years earlier were model Christians who loved the Lord and others 365 days a year. I have no doubt that both your rewards in Heaven are great!

Endorsements

Pastor Al has a HUGE heart for people bound in legalism and false doctrine. I know, because he helped me as I left the heresy of the Worldwide Church of God many years ago. I've watched him reach out to and help Mormons, Jehovah's Witnesses, and others. Unlike many, he researches these cult groups and learns to speak to them with facts and understanding instead of just spewing rhetoric. He literally connects with their hearts and minds such that real transformation can take place. This book is a glittering example of that. I highly recommend it to anyone who cares enough to see people set free from the Devil's religious lies.

- *Joel L. Rissinger*

Lead Pastor, Mill Pond Church and President, Rissinger Resource Group, LLC

"Books are powerful tools which unlock information, stir our imagination, and can even lead to transformation. In Mormonism Revisited, Al Stewart, disarms Mormonism and equips Christians to engage those who belong to the Church of the Latter-Day Saints. As a gifted evangelist, Pastor Al prepares us to

practically reach Mormons with the authentic message of the gospel."

- *Andrew Moroz, Teaching Pastor, Gospel Community Church – Rivermont, Lynchburg, Va.*

"My family and I spent 5 years in the LDS Church. And over that span I honestly thought it was God's one true Church. We are grateful to Pastor Al for providing us with the factual documented material that lead ultimately to our own investigation that the LDS Church was indeed not what it claimed. Our prayer now is that this book will provide the needed information to Mormon's so that like us, they can find their way to freedom in Christ"

- *Christopher Dufresne, former member of the LDS Church and Priesthood holder.*

Chapter Thirteen

Valuable Resources

There are many Books, DVD's and the like you can find on Mormonism. Here in my opinion is the *"cream of the crop"* so to speak, the materials I think that are most effective.

Book: Unveiling Grace, A very well written story told from the heart of a BYU Professor's entire family's journey to salvation in the Biblical Jesus. A powerful and emotional read that any thinking Mormon will appreciate. Author: Dr. Lynn Wilder, Publisher: Unveiling Grace, Contact: unveilingmormonism.com

Book: Changes in the Book of Mormon, Published by: Utah Lighthouse Ministry PO Box 1884 Salt Lake City, UT 84110 *(Sandra Tanner, considered the foremost expert on the Mormon Church today)*

DVD: DNA vs. the Book of Mormon

Available through Living Hope Ministries, www.livinghopeministries.info

DVD: Joseph Smith vs. The Bible

Available through Living Hope Ministries, www.livinghopeministries.info

DVD/Video: the Lost Book of Abraham, investigating a remarkable Mormon claim.

YouTube Link:
(*https://www.youtube.com/watch?v=rn1iGvXU0dI*)

Book: The Golden Bible: The Book of Mormon—Is It From God?   Author: M. T. Lamb   Publisher: Utah Lighthouse Ministry, PO Box 1884 Salt Lake City, UT 84110

Book: 7 Reasons We Left Mormonism, Authors: Dr. Lynn & Michael Wilder Publisher: Unveiling Grace, Contact: unvielingmormonism.com

Book: Leaving Mormonism, Why 4 Scholars Changed Their Minds, Authors; Dr. Lynn Wilder, Corey Miller, Latayne C. Scott & Vince Eccles. Contact: unvielingmormonism.com

About the Author

Rev. Al Stewart, D.D.

Currently makes his home in Forest, Virginia with his wife Dawn. He has two sons as well as a stepson. Al has pastored for over twenty-five years and is currently the Senior Pastor of Greater Grace Chapel in Lynchburg, Virginia (*greatergracechapel.com*). He is a native of Waterbury, Connecticut. Al attended Golden State School of Theology and received an honorary doctorate from Adonai International Christian University [A.I.C.U.] for his work specifically with both Jehovah's Witnesses and Mormons. He is currently ordained through Adonai International Fellowship Alliance [A.I.F.A.] and serves as its Mid-Atlantic Representative and V.P of Ministerial Affairs. He is also an ordained Police/Fire Chaplain through Shield of Faith Ministries and serves as the Asst. Chaplain of Post 16, American Legion of Lynchburg, Virginia, having served in West Germany in the U.S. Army from 1977-80.

Additional Books Available by Rev. Al Stewart

"Works Revisited" (Amazon/Createspace)

© 2017

Made in the USA
Columbia, SC
13 June 2018